OECD Development Co-operation Peer Reviews: Germany 2015

OECD
BETTER POLICIES FOR BETTER LIVES

This work is published under the responsibility of the Secretary-General of the OECD. The opinions expressed and arguments employed herein do not necessarily reflect the official views of OECD member countries.

This document and any map included herein are without prejudice to the status of or sovereignty over any territory, to the delimitation of international frontiers and boundaries and to the name of any territory, city or area.

Please cite this publication as:
OECD (2015), *OECD Development Co-operation Peer Reviews: Germany 2015*, OECD Publishing, Paris.
http://dx.doi.org/10.1787/9789264246133-en

ISBN 978-92-64-24612-6 (print)
ISBN 978-92-64-24613-3 (PDF)

Series: OECD Development Co-operation Peer Reviews
ISSN 2309-7124 (print)
ISSN 2309-7132 (online)

The statistical data for Israel are supplied by and under the responsibility of the relevant Israeli authorities. The use of such data by the OECD is without prejudice to the status of the Golan Heights, East Jerusalem and Israeli settlements in the West Bank under the terms of international law.

Corrigenda to OECD publications may be found on line at: *www.oecd.org/about/publishing/corrigenda.htm*.

Conducting the peer review

The OECD Development Assistance Committee (DAC) conducts periodic reviews of the individual development co-operation efforts of DAC members. The policies and programmes of each member are critically examined approximately once every four or five years. Five members are examined annually. The OECD Development Co-operation Directorate provides analytical support, and develops and maintains, in close consultation with the Committee, the methodology and analytical framework – known as the Reference Guide – within which the peer reviews are undertaken.

The objectives of DAC peer reviews are to improve the quality and effectiveness of development co-operation policies and systems, and to promote good development partnerships for better impact on poverty reduction and sustainable development in developing countries. DAC peer reviews assess the performance of a given member, not just that of its development co-operation agency, and examine both policy and implementation. They take an integrated, system-wide perspective on the development co-operation and humanitarian assistance activities of the member under review.

The peer review is prepared by a team, consisting of representatives of the Secretariat working with officials from two DAC members who are designated as "examiners". The country under review provides a memorandum setting out the main developments in its policies and programmes. Then the Secretariat and the examiners visit the capital to interview officials, parliamentarians, as well as civil society and NGO representatives of the donor country to obtain a first-hand insight into current issues surrounding the development co-operation efforts of the member concerned. Field visits assess how members are implementing the major DAC policies, principles and concerns, and review operations in recipient countries, particularly with regard to poverty reduction, sustainability, gender equality and other aspects of participatory development, and local aid co-ordination. During the field visit, the team meets with representatives of the partner country's administration, parliamentarians, civil society and other development partners.

The Secretariat then prepares a draft report on the member's development co-operation which is the basis for the DAC review meeting at the OECD. At this meeting senior officials from the member under review respond to questions formulated by the Committee in association with the examiners.

This review contains the main findings and recommendations of the Development Assistance Committee and the report of the Secretariat. It was prepared with examiners from Canada and Japan for the peer review of Germany on 16 September 2015.

Table of contents

Tables

Figures

Boxes

Abbreviations and acronyms

BMAS	Bundesministerium für Arbeit und Soziales, Federal Ministry for Labour and Social Affairs
BMUB	Bundesministerium für Umwelt, Naturschutz, Bau und Reaktorsicherheit - Germany's Federal Ministry for the Environment, Nature Conservation, and Nuclear Safety
BMZ	Bundesministerium für wirtschaftliche Zusammenarbeit und Entwicklung - Germany's Federal Ministry for Economic Co-operation and Development
CDU	Christian Democratic Union
CSO	Civil society organisation
CSU	Christian Social Union
DAC	Development Assistance Committee (OECD)
DED	Deutscher Entwicklungsdienst - German Development Service
DEG	Deutsche Investitions- und Entwicklungsgesellschaft - German Investment and Development Corporation
DEval	German Institute for Development Evaluation
DIE	Deutsches Institut für Entwicklungspolitik - German Development Institute
EU	European Union
FFO	Federal Foreign Office
KfW	Kreditanstalt für Wiederaufbau, KfW Development Bank
GIZ	Deutsche Gesellschaft für Internationale Zusammenarbeit
GNI	Gross national income
GTZ	Gesellschaft für Technische Zusammenarbeit - German technical Co-operation
IKI	International Climate Initiative
IKLU	Initiative for Climate and Environmental Protection
LDC	Least developed country
NGO	Non-governmental organisation
OCHA	UN Office for the Co-ordination of Humanitarian Affairs
ODA	Official development assistance
OOF	Other official flows
PPP	Public-private partnership
SDG	Sustainable Development Goal
SDP	Social Democratic Party
UN	United Nations
UNFCCC	United Nations Framework Convention on Climate Change

Signs used:

EUR	Euro
USD	United States dollars
( )	Secretariat estimate in whole or part
-	(Nil)
0.0	Negligible
..	Not available
...	Not available separately, but included in total
n.a.	Not applicable
p	Provisional

Slight discrepancies in totals are due to rounding.

Annual average exchange rate: 1 EUR = USD

2009	2010	2011	2012	2013
0.7181	0.7550	0.7192	0.7780	0.7532

Germany's aid at a glance

GERMANY

Gross Bilateral ODA, 2012-13 average, unless otherwise shown

Net ODA	2012	2013	2014	Change 2013/14
Current (USD m)	12 939	14 228	16 249	14.2%
Constant (2013 USD m)	13 639	14 228	15 940	12.0%
In Euro (million)	10 067	10 717	12 247	14.3%
ODA/GNI	0.37%	0.38%	0.41%	
Bilateral share	66%	66%	70%	

Top Ten Recipients of Gross ODA (USD million)	
1 China (People's Republic of)	682
2 India	610
3 Afghanistan	532
4 Democratic Republic of the Congo	344
5 Côte d'Ivoire	262
6 Kenya	235
7 Turkey	219
8 Egypt	216
9 Syrian Arab Republic	209
10 Brazil	208
Memo: Share of gross bilateral ODA	
Top 5 recipients	22%
Top 10 recipients	32%
Top 20 recipients	43%

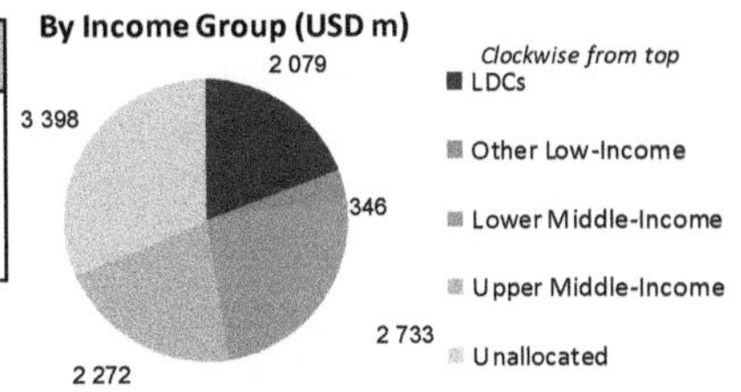

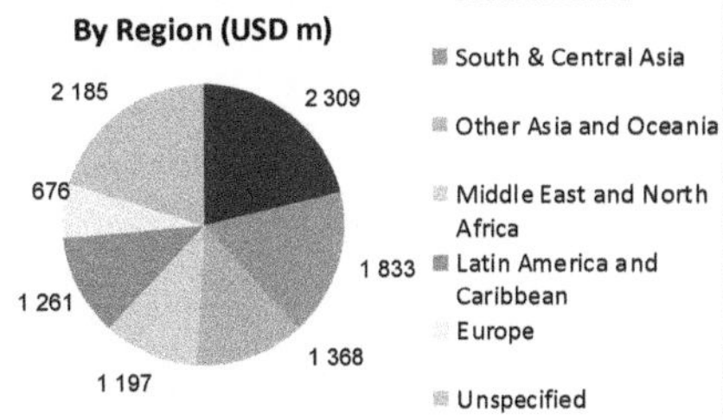

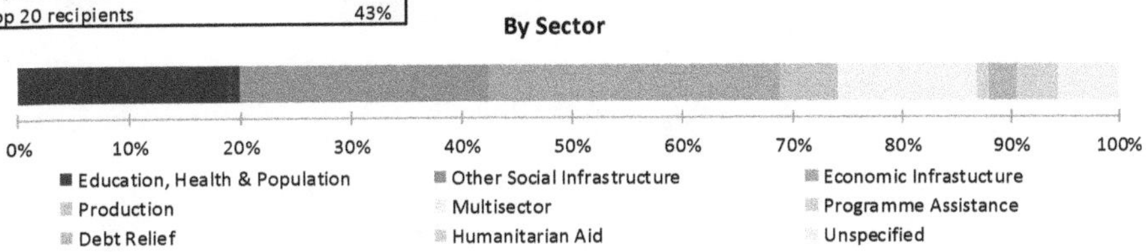

Source: OECD-DAC; www.oecd.org/dac/stats

Figure 0.1 Germany's implementation of 2010 peer review recommendations

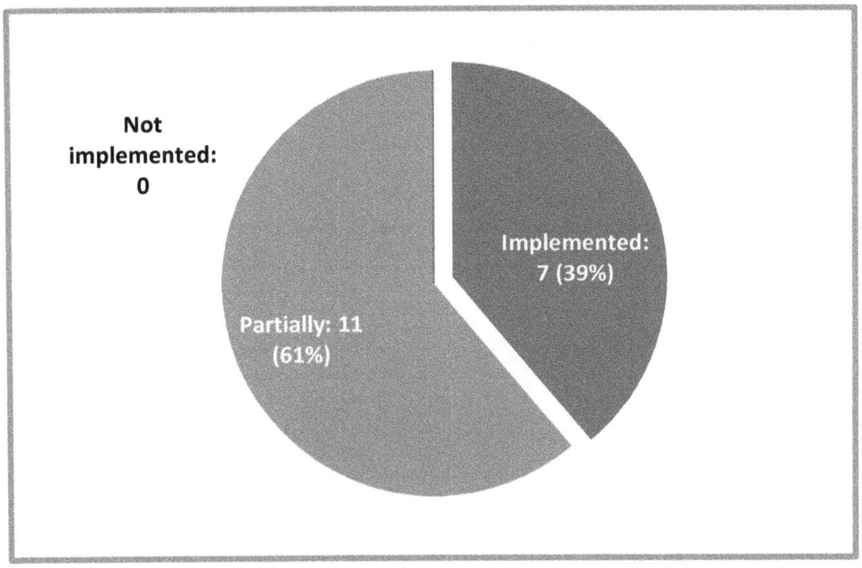

Context of Germany's peer review

Political and economic context

With a population of 82.6 million, in 2014 Germany was the fourth largest economy in the world in terms of nominal gross domestic product. As a global economic power, Germany participates in many international bodies, including the G8 and G20, and is a key member of the European Union (EU).

General elections in 2013 were won by the Christian Democratic Union/Christian Social Union of Chancellor Angela Merkel. Merkel's party reached a coalition agreement with the main opposition party – the Social Democrats – to form a grand coalition. The Coalition Treaty, adopted in December 2013, establishes the German policy framework. As set out in the treaty, Germany considers development as a global structural policy and wants to make globalisation sustainable and fair for all people. It therefore actively promotes a comprehensive 2030 Agenda that applies at both domestic and international levels. The coalition treaty also reiterates Germany's commitment to the United Nations (UN) of giving 0.7% of its gross national income as official development assistance, although it lacks a timetable to reach this target.

German leadership has taken shape in recent years in response to the crises affecting the Euro zone and the region. Germany aims to prevent these crises from escalating and to promote an international system of rules, working closely with international partners and institutions. At the same time, its development co-operation objectives are to defeat hunger and poverty; strengthen democracy and the rule of law; and encourage the establishment of socially and ecologically orientated market economies. These broad objectives were translated into eight priority areas in a Charter for the Future which was unveiled by Federal Chancellor Angela Merkel and Development Minister Gerd Müller in November 2014, following wide consultations with all German stakeholders.

Long-term and continuous economic growth driven by the social market economy underpins the federal government's economic policy. Germany's economy has proven remarkably resilient in the face of recent crises. Unemployment has reached its lowest levels since unification, reflecting the ambitious reforms of the past decade, and the current account surplus remains large. However, a number of challenges are on the horizon. The OECD's 2014 economic survey of Germany projects that growth will fall over the next 20 years because of demographic changes. The share of low-paying jobs has risen considerably. Public investment is low and government spending on key services to support inclusive growth, notably childcare, needs to rise further. Finally, with no new policies, targets for CO_2 emission reductions will be missed.

Sources: "Charter for the Future - One world, Our Responsibility", BMZ, Bonn; CDU/CSU/SPD (2014), *Shaping Germany's Future – Coalition treaty between CDU/CSU and SPD, 18th legislative period,* unofficial translation, available at www.kas.de/wf/doc/kas_36853-544-2-30.pdf?140820093605; OECD (2014), *OECD Economic Surveys: Germany 2014*, OECD Publishing, Paris, http://dx.doi.org/10.1787/eco_surveys-deu-2014-en.

The DAC's main findings and recommendations

1 Towards a comprehensive German development effort

Indicator: The member has a broad, strategic approach to development and financing for development beyond aid. This is reflected in overall policies, co-ordination within its government system, and operations.

Main findings

Germany is a prominent player in promoting sustainable development on the international stage. Backed by strong political commitment and sound cross-government strategies for global engagement, it uses its position strategically to engage in key areas for development. In particular, it took the opportunity of its Presidency of the G7 in 2015 to encourage strong commitments on the 2030 and climate change agendas and enhance action in other important areas such as women's entrepreneurship, financial market regulation, taxation, trade barriers, and responsible supply chains. Germany is also involved in partnerships targeting global public goods with a number of emerging economies.

Since 2013, Germany has advanced the principles of universality, shared responsibility and transparent monitoring in the design of the Sustainable Development Goals (SDGs), to be adopted in September 2015 at the United Nations General Assembly. Leading by example, the Federal Ministry for Economic Co-operation and Development (BMZ) issued a "Charter for the Future" in 2014, which sets out its vision for contributing to sustainable development at home and abroad. Germany's consistent approach makes it well placed to play a strong role in promoting the implementation of the SDGs, in particular among the OECD members.

Germany's approach to policy coherence for development is an organic part of its policy making, a feature that is now translated into its broad, holistic approach to the 2030 Agenda. Germany has had a National Sustainable Development Strategy in place since 2002. The government plans to update it by second half of 2016 to reflect the SDGs so that it provides the framework for implementing the 2030 Agenda within Germany. Prioritising a limited number of strategic areas where there are win-win opportunities for Germany and developing countries would help to work effectively on issues of common interest across the government – at home and abroad.

BMZ is responsible for promoting policy coherence for development across government. Its seat in Cabinet allows it to scrutinise every policy from a development perspective, and its recent strengthening reinforces this ability. Looking forward, Germany is well prepared to address the universal and integrated 2030 Agenda, which will require intensified collaboration across government, led at the highest level: the National Sustainable Development Strategy falls under the competence of the Federal Chancellery, and the State Secretaries' Committee for Sustainable Development monitors and reports on its implementation.

Updating the National Sustainable Development Strategy is an opportunity to conduct forward-looking analysis and identify emerging areas of incoherence more systematically. In addition to using the expertise of German research institutes, Germany can also draw on its dialogue with partner countries and the political analyses conducted by BMZ and the German embassies, which have the potential to identify areas of competing interests. Communicating its efforts and learning from the results more systematically would also help BMZ to promote coherence for development more effectively.

Germany is at the forefront in using public development finance to leverage engagement and investment from the private sector for sustainable development, seeking to build synergies among the various German stakeholders at home and in partner countries. It mobilises a wide range of instruments – from concessional loans to risk capital provision and guarantees – and has developed some innovative approaches for engaging with local, German and international companies. Germany also stands out for its level of commitment and innovative approaches to financing climate change activities. It is well equipped to support green investments effectively, which it does increasingly in middle-income countries.

Recommendation

1.1 In updating its National Sustainable Development Strategy, Germany should prioritise a few areas of domestic or foreign policy where it can address incoherence or achieve greater coherence with development benefits. Monitoring progress towards more coherent policies will be required.

2 Germany's vision and policies for development co-operation

Indicator: Clear political directives, policies and strategies shape the member's development co-operation and are in line with international commitments and guidance.

Main findings

The Charter for the Future provides an overarching, value-driven vision for development, which seeks to advance sustainable development as both a domestic and a global issue. While the Charter also provides a broad basis for development co-operation, its strategic messages and commitments constitute an important input into implementing the 2030 Agenda. In implementing the 2030 Agenda, the German government should clarify the hierarchy of priorities, including the three Special Initiatives launched in 2014 to address hunger, refugees and the Middle East crisis. Looking forward, BMZ plans to use the implementation of the SDGs to enhance whole-of-government approaches in partner countries.

Germany aims to reduce poverty, with a special focus on the poorest countries, especially in Africa. It promotes democracy and good governance, social and environmental responsibility and a market-based economy. The poverty focus of its development co-operation is underpinned by clear statements and solid guidance. A strong policy framework also supports engagement in fragile contexts.

BMZ's allocations are context-based, with the mix of instruments tailored to each situation. In differentiating its development co-operation approaches according to the characteristics of each partner country, Germany is well positioned for the future, since context-specific approaches will become more important to deal effectively with a broader agenda.

Germany's allocations criteria and instruments are not fully aligned with its political intentions. In particular, the "Catalogue of Criteria" - one instrument among others - that guides its bilateral allocations emphasises partner countries' good governance and effectiveness as criteria for German support. This may contradict Germany's intention to focus more on fragile countries, where governance tends to be lacking. Similarly, Germany's portfolio of loans results in a disconnect between its stated focus on the poorest countries and the volume of German ODA going to middle income countries. Finally, Germany's aim to use the most effective and efficient type of intervention may be hampered by the system of fixed, separate budget lines for technical and financial co-operation. Separate budget lines also make it more difficult to respond to programme demands and evolving situations, obstacles that the implementing agencies are trying to overcome pragmatically.

Meanwhile as there are now more development co-operation staff in embassies, they are in a better position to strengthen synergies between the bilateral programme and projects of non-state actors which receive direct funding from parliament. This would reinforce the overall consistency of Germany's co-operation in the field.

BMZ has taken steps to engage more strategically with multilateral organisations and vertical funds, commissioning a study of its co-operation with 30 different organisations. The findings will help BMZ to drive reforms of, and to review its resource allocations to, these organisations. As an active player in the multilateral system reform process, Germany is constructively involved on governing boards so as to help multilateral organisations fulfil their mandates more effectively.

Climate change is increasingly a core priority for Germany. It is well embedded in the programme, both thematically and as a cross-cutting dimension. Germany is also taking serious steps to address gender equality with appropriate guidance and tools. BMZ should clarify how to deal with other cross-cutting issues. Recognising that it is hard to follow up effectively on many cross-cutting issues at once, a pragmatic solution would be to prioritise issues according to each national context. At the same time, assigning senior-level champions to advocate for each issue, backed by adequate resources, would help to implement selected cross-cutting issues effectively across all sectors as well as in policy dialogue. This is particularly relevant for gender equality, as BMZ is developing an implementation plan for its gender strategy.

Recommendations

2.1 To inform development co-operation programming within government and guide partners, Germany should translate the Charter for the Future into an operational framework.

2.2 Germany needs to bring its allocation criteria and instruments in alignment with its policy.

2.3 BMZ should match its commitment to mainstreaming gender equality and other cross-cutting issues with the leadership, resources and tools needed to deliver.

3 Allocating Germany's official development assistance

Indicator: The member's international and national commitments drive aid volume and allocations.

Main findings

Germany's official development assistance (ODA) is at an all-time high – at USD 16.25 billion (provisional 2014 figures), equivalent to 0.41% of gross national income (GNI). This represents a 12% increase in real terms from 2013. Germany is the 3rd largest DAC donor in terms of volume and the 10th in terms of its ODA as a percentage of GNI.

Germany's commitment to meet the UN target of allocating 0.7% of its GNI as ODA is enshrined in the 2013 government coalition treaty. The government has announced increases of EUR 10.3 billion in the aid budget, to take effect between 2014 and 2019. However, Germany's current economic growth rate means that the planned increases will only maintain ODA at 0.4% as a percentage of GNI, which is still a long way off the 0.7% target. With its strong economy, and building on the momentum of the Charter for the Future, Germany is well placed to set a more ambitious plan with time-bound milestones for meeting its international ODA/GNI commitment. This would also be in line with the EU commitment to achieve the 0.7% target within the time frame of the 2030 Agenda, as announced at the Addis Ababa Conference on Financing for Development in July 2015.

Germany's political commitment to focus on the poorest countries, especially in Africa, is only partly reflected in its bilateral ODA allocations. In 2013, 32% of Germany's total bilateral allocable ODA went to Africa, while 34% went to Asia. At the same time, only 27% of bilateral allocable ODA went to least-developed and other low-income countries, while 73% went to middle-income countries. These discrepancies between political intentions and actual ODA spending result from the fact that the allocation criteria only apply to BMZ's budget funds. KfW, the German Development Bank, is not bound by these criteria when using its own resources to provide less concessional funding. Loans accounted for 34% of gross bilateral ODA disbursements in 2014, largely to middle-income countries.

While Germany is well equipped to use different instruments in different contexts, the share of German bilateral ODA allocated to the least developed and other low-income countries is decreasing. This trend means Germany cannot make good on its promise to join collective efforts to reverse the declining trend of ODA to these countries, a commitment reaffirmed at the DAC High Level Meeting in 2014 and the Addis Ababa Conference.

Since 2010, Germany has reduced from 55 to 50 the number of partner countries with which it has a full development co-operation programme. It continues to co-operate with another 29 countries on thematic issues. This stronger focus has, however, not led to greater ODA concentration because there has been an increase in funds which are not allocated geographically. DAC data on Germany's country programmable aid confirms that nearly half of German bilateral ODA is unavailable for programming at partner country level: 22% of bilateral aid is unallocated while imputed student costs, humanitarian aid, debt relief and administrative costs combined account for 24%.

Sector allocations reflect Germany's policy focus on poverty reduction, governance, economic growth, and environment. Germany stands out for its emphasis on climate change. The share of its bilateral aid focusing on climate change mitigation and adaptation reached 28% (while the DAC country average is 16%).

In 2013, Germany allocated 29% of total ODA as core contributions to multilateral organisations. It channelled a further 7% of its bilateral ODA for specific projects implemented by multilateral organisations as non-core contributions. Although total gross ODA allocated to the multilateral system has declined over the last five years, Germany is constructively involved, giving priority to core contributions in accordance with its strategy to help multilateral organisations deliver their mandate effectively. Recently, Germany increased its earmarked non-core contributions to support multi-donor thematic funds, mainly for responding to humanitarian crisis. This is good practice, helping co-ordinate more effective responses.

Recommendations

3.1 Germany should set a time-bound path for increasing its aid volumes to meet the 0.7% ODA to GNI commitment.

3.2 As the development co-operation budget grows, Germany should prioritise increasing support to least developed countries in order to reach the 0.20% ODA/GNI target within the timeframe of the 2030 Agenda, as agreed within the EU context.

4 Managing Germany's development co-operation

Indicator: The member's approach to how it organises and manages its development co-operation is fit for purpose.

Main findings

Germany has taken further steps to streamline its complex institutional system, in particular by clarifying the mandates of the various stakeholders and by merging three technical co-operation agencies.

BMZ now has the main policy steering and oversight role for German development co-operation. This, together with its enhanced capacity, means there is a better balance between policy and implementation at headquarters and in the field. However, BMZ's business model does not enable it to support context-based, responsive approaches in the field in the most effective way. Processes are time consuming and the resulting delays undermine implementation in partner countries. Streamlining systems and procedures at headquarters would help to reduce staff workloads and re-allocate personnel where they are most needed.

Implementing the 2030 Agenda makes it even more important for BMZ to play its steering function to the full, developing synergies and sharing lessons with other ministries as well as federal states and local governments more systematically. This implies considering which organisational arrangement best support whole-of-government approaches. As regards implementation, the fact that Germany's implementing agencies are being commissioned by ministries other than BMZ to implement programmes can help ensure consistency in Germany's overall approach to development.

With more development co-operation staff posted in embassies, BMZ and the Federal Foreign Office will need to look at ways to delegate greater authority to the field, building on the experience gathered in the two-year pilot launched in 2014 in eight partner countries. Improving the information loop across the German system would reduce transaction costs and facilitate consultation, oversight and decision-making processes. Such improvements would help address the concerns raised by some partners that it takes too long to get decisions and approvals from headquarters.

The merger of three technical co-operation agencies into GIZ is bearing fruit in terms of efficiency and strategic coherence, while the comparative advantages of each instrument have been retained and their use sharpened. KfW has also undergone significant reform to adapt to new instruments and deliver the programme more effectively and efficiently.

In partner countries, the various German institutions, instruments and tools work coherently, seeking synergies with programmes designed jointly at the sector level. Operational co-ordination is aided by the clearer division of labour between BMZ and the implementing agencies, the establishment of country teams and – in most partner countries – the fact that GIZ and KfW offices are located in a common "German House". Flexibility and good information sharing, supported by clear guidance from headquarters, are essential for this to work effectively.

The German implementing agencies encourage creativity and this translates into a number of innovative approaches for making the most of opportunities as they arise. While GIZ is largely decentralised, KfW should consider the pros and cons of delegating further authority to country offices, backed up by additional human resources and greater empowerment for local managers. This will help the agency to adjust to the demands for decentralisation which is likely to increase as more countries develop their capacity to engage with development partners.

The German institutions are making efforts to match their staffing to needs. BMZ has managed a substantial increase in staff, while the implementing agencies have improved opportunities for professional development. The fact that heads of co-operation positions are strategic and require high-calibre staff should be recognised in career pathways and training access.

Recommendations

4.1 To implement the 2030 Agenda, BMZ needs to fulfil its steering function for German development co-operation to the full. Streamlining communication across the entire system would facilitate BMZ's oversight while reducing transaction costs.

4.2 BMZ should speed up its programming process and ensure procedures are flexible enough to respond to conditions on the ground, without compromising quality and integrity.

5 Germany's development co-operation delivery and partnerships

Indicator: The member's approach to how it delivers its programme leads to quality assistance in partner countries, maximising the impact of its support, as defined in Busan.

Main findings

Bilateral negotiations with partner country governments shape Germany's development co-operation programmes. While Germany's budgeting process enables multi-year commitments, BMZ does not share long-term spending information systematically with partner countries. The new country strategy format could enable long-term strategic planning and predictability for both Germany and its partners, but to date less than half have been finished.

The introduction of Special Initiatives reflects Germany's high-level political commitment to addressing pressing needs. With these initiatives, resources can be allocated through any channel of German development co-operation. This is a major change to BMZ's way of working, which gives the ministry the opportunity to choose the most appropriate instrument and work with the most relevant partners. In taking this approach forward, the challenge for BMZ is to make the most of the flexibility inherent in these initiatives without compromising the coherence of country programmes with separate planning and reporting requirements.

Germany's use of partner country systems varies across sectors and modalities. Germany does its best to align project-based assistance with country systems by integrating projects into programme-based approaches. Additional safeguards are included in cases where there are serious concerns about fiduciary risks. While this approach is justified, it is important to identify jointly with the government and other partners priority issues for strengthening country systems and to build the necessary trust for gradually making greater use of these systems, in line with the Busan commitment. Germany has made progress in untying more ODA: in 2013, 80% of its total bilateral aid was untied, up from 75% in 2010. This in part reflects progress in untying technical co-operation, which rose from 48% to 57% during the same period.

Germany is moving towards a more comprehensive approach to capacity development, combining both technical and financial co-operation. While technical co-operation is appreciated by partners, visits to Kenya and Mozambique show that partner structures could be used more in programme implementation. This would help build national capacity and ensure sustainability.

Germany remains committed to effective development co-operation principles, demonstrated by its collaboration with other development partners. It increasingly takes a lead role in policy dialogue and co-ordination, where its solid expertise is valued by its partners. Germany is therefore well placed to promote country-led efforts to enhance mutual accountability, essential for shaping effective partnerships for implementing the SDGs.

Germany values the role of civil society and provides 8% of its total net ODA to and through NGOs. Political foundations and the two main church-based development organisations have separate budget allocations and, while subject to strict auditing and monitoring procedures, have wide programming autonomy. Project-based funding to all other NGOs through Engagement Global, however, has high transaction costs as many small-scale projects are funded. In refining its strategy and tools for engaging with civil society, BMZ might want to consider how the role of Engagement Global and the use of different standards for various types of organisations can be adapted so as to best strengthen civil society in developing countries while reducing transaction costs.

Conflict sensitivity and consideration of factors exacerbating fragility are well embedded in BMZ's country strategies. More flexible procedures help to implement programmes in difficult and low-capacity contexts. Preparing country strategies through a whole-of-government approach would allow for greater coherence and help capitalise on synergies among different German actors.

Recommendations

5.1 To strengthen the predictability of its programmes and strategic planning, BMZ should speed up the process of finalising its country strategies.

5.2 Germany needs to identify ways of increasing gradually its use of partner country systems, working closely with other development partners.

5.3 To maximise the impact of its support to civil society and reduce transaction costs, BMZ should consider how to provide multi-year programme funding rather than supporting small, stand-alone projects.

6 Results and accountability of Germany's development co-operation

Indicator: The member plans and manages for results, learning, transparency and accountability.

Main findings

BMZ has strengthened its approach to results within individual programmes, which is now embedded in the commissioning process with implementing agencies. A results matrix, which provides the basis for GIZ and KfW programming and reporting, helps to clarify expectations and focus attention on what programmes can realistically achieve. In line with the Busan commitment to use partner countries' own results frameworks, these results matrices draw on indicators and data from partner countries, minimising the need for additional data collection. In addition, most technical co-operation programmes include a specific component for strengthening partner countries' monitoring and evaluation systems. BMZ is taking stock of its approach to results-based financing, which could provide useful lessons for other development agencies.

While GIZ and KfW use results information routinely for improving programme management, BMZ is not yet able to make full use of results information and evidence from other sources for strategic planning and communication. BMZ now needs to work out how to aggregate reporting from individual activities so as to use information on results consistently for policy, planning, budgeting and communication. Embedding a results culture within BMZ will require steering from the top.

Like other DAC members, Germany needs to consolidate its reporting on results by explaining better what drives outcomes and impacts in the context of wider development processes. Results matrices in programmes provide a good basis for meaningful analysis from activities to impact. BMZ can use them to measure how German development co-operation contributes to support developing country partners in achieving their own results.

BMZ has allocated more resources for evaluation, notably with the creation of the German Institute for Development Evaluation (DEval). It still needs to work through some specific aspects of the new set up, including practical implications for the role and responsibilities of the ministry's own evaluation unit. Realising DEval's potential will require strong leadership, strategic planning, adequate funding and effective reporting lines which guarantee impartiality and independence. While GIZ and KfW both have reinforced their independent evaluation of individual projects, the link between evaluations and results frameworks is not yet in place. In partner countries, Germany does not conduct periodic portfolio reviews. Such reviews could be used to feed experience of what works into future programming choices.

The overall coherence and efficiency of Germany's approach to knowledge management needs to be consolidated. While implementing agencies have systems in place to disseminate evaluation findings and share experience, BMZ needs to ensure that it manages and uses this knowledge both centrally and in its implementing agencies. It also needs to make evidence available systematically, including for staff seconded to embassies in developing countries.

Recognising the importance of transparency for accountability, Germany has set up a dedicated web-based transparency portal for increasing public information on individual projects. To comply with the Busan common, open standard on transparency by 2015, however, Germany will need to publish more detailed information. This includes meeting information needs of developing countries, such as on results achieved and future funding. Ministries other than BMZ also need to be more transparent about their action.

Although BMZ uses a range of different communication tools, it is not yet able to aggregate reporting from individual activities into an overall narrative describing how successful development co-operation is. The Charter for the Future has created a platform for dialogue that BMZ can use for stepping up its communication efforts.

Recommendations

6.1 Drawing on its experience with programme results matrices, BMZ should adopt a results-based management system which is fit for its needs of improving decision making and being accountable.

6.2 BMZ needs to work through how the evaluation set up functions in practice to ensure it gets and makes full use of the independent evidence needed to drive the overall programme more strategically.

7 Germany's humanitarian assistance

Indicator: The member contributes to minimising impact of shocks and crises; and saves lives, alleviates suffering and maintains human dignity in crisis and disaster settings.

Main findings

Germany's humanitarian assistance is based in the Federal Foreign Office and is complemented by:

- BMZ's development and transitional aid
- the Special Initiatives, which deal partly with the causes of, and fall-out from, humanitarian crises.

The 2013 government coalition agreement includes a new political commitment to humanitarian aid. There have also been significant improvements in the quality of the humanitarian aid programme.

The findings of the 2012 joint BMZ/Foreign Office evaluation of the German humanitarian programme have led to a clearer division of labour between the two organisations; this is a positive development.

Building on the division of labour agreement, the Foreign Office has a put in place a new, strategic approach to humanitarian aid, covering both response and preparedness. This new approach has allowed the Foreign Office's humanitarian programme to focus on quality partnerships with the humanitarian community, and to target areas where Germany can clearly add value. For example, Germany added value to its funding for Syria by hosting the Berlin Conference on the Syrian Refugee Situation, which looked at how the international community can support the refugees and the neighbouring countries in a better and more sustainable way.

Germany is also making serious efforts to improve humanitarian preparedness, both through its own programming and on the global stage.

The Foreign Office has the right tools and supportive, strategic partnerships with humanitarian organisations; these help Germany to facilitate an effective response in both rapid onset crises and complex emergencies. Germany is also serious about co-ordination with other donors, both on global policy issues and in the field.

There are systems in place to ensure that early warning leads to early action; this has proved useful in sudden onset and escalating crises, such as the 2011 Kenyan drought.

The Foreign Office actively promotes the participation of affected people in its partners' programmes; this is good practice.

There is good strategic co-ordination among Germany's humanitarian actors – including NGOs and the various parts of government involved in humanitarian response. Germany is also raising awareness of civil military principle within its own military and other nations' peacekeeping forces.

Staff in the field, and in Berlin, are seen as knowledgeable on humanitarian issues. A range of good practice innovations, such as staff exchanges with humanitarian agencies, have been developed.

Partner reporting is focused on results and learning; field staff are also involved in monitoring, where security conditions permit. However, there are no indicators to support Germany's own progress as a good humanitarian donor. In addition, BMZ and the Foreign Office could make better use of partners' communications materials. Germany informed the Committee that the Federal Foreign Office is introducing a new monitoring and evaluation system and a communication policy to address these issues.

The humanitarian budget has increased, but still represents only 6.5% of Germany's ODA; there is therefore scope for additional budget increases to demonstrate that Germany is sharing the global humanitarian assistance burden.

There is a lack of clarity about how BMZ's transition strategy and tools will be implemented, including the Special Initiatives. This is limiting Germany's ability to support systematically coherent and holistic responses in protracted crises and transition situations. Germany is currently reviewing its approach to recovery and transition, a positive move to improve its humanitarian response.

Recommendation

7.1 To ensure a holistic German humanitarian response, BMZ needs to clarify how its transitional funding and Special Initiatives will be used, and make these funds more predictable and easier to access.

Secretariat's report

Chapter 1: Towards a comprehensive German development effort

Global development issues

Germany is engaging in development at the international level, especially in post-2015 processes and in tackling climate change. It is also involved in partnerships targeting global public goods – such as peace and security – with a number of emerging economies. Taking advantage of the government position on post-2015 and BMZ's Charter for the Future, Germany is well positioned to play a stronger role in promoting the implementation of the Sustainable Development Goals, at home and abroad. Its presidency of the G7 in 2015 offers a key opportunity for doing so.

Germany is active at the global level to support development

Germany is a prominent player in promoting sustainable development on the international stage. Backed by strong political commitment and sound cross-government strategies for global engagement, it is increasingly involved in shaping the global development agenda, using its position strategically in a number of key international arenas. Adopting a forward-looking vision, Germany has developed a cross-government strategy for global engagement to shape its partnerships with emerging economies in key policy areas: peace and security; human rights and the rule of law; economic and financial policy; resources, food and energy; employment, social affairs and health; and development and sustainability (FFO, 2012).

Germany's involvement in the inter-governmental negotiations on the post-2015 agenda provides a good illustration of its approach. Germany's former President was a member of the High-Level Panel of Eminent Persons on the Post-2015 Development Agenda convened by the UN Secretary-General in 2012. The German government also engaged strategically in the next phase, laying out its key positions for this agenda in August 2013 and detailing them in December 2014 in Cabinet decisions (Federal Government, 2014). Germany's post-2015 position is ambitious and guided by the principles of universality, shared responsibility and transparent monitoring. In order to lead by example, the Federal Ministry for Economic Co-operation and Development (BMZ) has published a "Charter for the Future: One World – Our Responsibility" in which it sets out its vision for contributing to sustainable development at home and abroad (BMZ, 2014a). Building on this charter, Germany is using its 2015 Presidency of the G7 to promote the 2030 Agenda and a set of key development priorities, in particular climate change as well as decent working conditions and social and environmental standards.[1]

Climate change is an area where Germany shows constant leadership in both global and local contexts. Its advocacy is backed by a high level of commitment to financing climate change activities in partner countries. Germany took the lead in supporting the capitalisation of the Green Climate Fund, for example. It also outlined progress and options for long-term climate finance at the G7 leaders' summit in June 2015, aiming for a global agreement to curb climate change at the 21st session of the Conference of the Parties to the United Nations Framework Convention on Climate Change in December 2015.

Policy coherence for development

Indicator: Domestic policies support or do not harm developing countries

Driven by its policy commitment to the 2030 Agenda, Germany is enhancing efforts to ensure its domestic and foreign policies support sustainable development. It can consolidate progress further by prioritising cross-governmental goals within the national sustainable development strategy, by making full use of the institutional set-up and by learning more from past efforts on policy coherence for development.

Germany's commitment to policy coherence reflects its strong policy focus on sustainable development

Germany has been advocating for policy coherence for development within the European Union (EU), the OECD and other international organisations for many years.[2] At home, the Federal Government continues to give high priority to this agenda. As is stated in the Coalition Treaty, Germany is committed to work better across government in order to make government policy more development-oriented (CDU/CSU/SPD, 2014).[3]

Germany's approach to policy coherence for development is an organic part of policy making, a feature that is now translated into its broad, holistic approach to the 2030 Agenda. Germany has had a National Sustainable Development Strategy in place since 2002, which it has updated regularly. The strategy serves as the guide for a comprehensive political agenda that addresses Germany's responsibility for an economically, ecologically and socially sound development for all generations. It sets out quantified goals for 21 key areas related to sustainable development, covering both the domestic and international agenda - the latter goals being approached so far through development co-operation and by opening markets. The latest progress report on the strategy was adopted by the Federal Government in February 2012. It states that the Federal Government will weave the topic of sustainability into its foreign policy to an even greater degree in the future (Federal Government, 2012a).

Germany plans to update the strategy by 2016 to reflect the sustainable development goals (SDGs) that will be adopted in September 2015 at the UN General Assembly. This will be an opportunity to translate the vision provided by the Charter for the Future into concrete objectives at home and abroad and develop an implementation plan. Given that the SDGs are very comprehensive, this plan should include a prioritised, time-bound coherence agenda setting strategic cross-governmental goals for national policies in areas with potential development benefit as well as for global public goods.[4]

Mechanisms are in place to ensure policies support sustainable development

In line with its strategic approach to promoting sustainable development, Germany's Federal Government has put in place mechanisms for ensuring policy co-ordination and coherence in a number of key public policies. As an overarching structure, the Federal Committee of State Secretaries for Sustainable Development, comprising permanent state secretaries from all federal ministries, meets regularly in the Chancellor's office. This committee is responsible for all important decisions concerning the sustainability strategy. Inter-ministerial committees have also been established to address specific issues such as migration, food security and climate change – an area which involves close collaboration between BMZ and the Ministry for the Environment, Nature Conservation, Building and Nuclear Safety (BMUB, hereafter the Ministry for Environment). A specific committee, co-chaired by BMZ and the Ministry for Environment, prepared the Government position on post-2015. These mechanisms have already produced some good results – some of which are listed in the European Union (EU) report on coherence for development (EC, 2013).[5]

BMZ is responsible for promoting policy coherence for development across the German government and the EU.[6] Together with the Ministry for Environment, it has been steering the post-2015 process within government and with external stakeholders. Having a seat in Cabinet allows BMZ to scrutinise every policy from a development perspective; its recent strengthening makes it even better equipped to analyse the effects of domestic policies on developing countries (Chapter 4).

Looking forward, Germany is well positioned to address the SDGs as a government-wide agenda supported by extensive cross-government collaboration. The National Sustainable Development Strategy, which will provide the framework for the implementation of the 2030 Agenda, falls under the competence of the Federal Chancellery. All ministries are involved in shaping and implementing the strategy: the Federal Cabinet adopts changes in, and further develops, the Strategy; meanwhile the States Secretaries' Committee for Sustainable Development, which is chaired by the Head of the Federal Chancellery and in which all ministries are represented, is in charge of progress reports and monitors the development of the sustainability indicators (Federal Government, 2012b). Germany's experience in bringing together ministries to promote global development may be useful to other OECD members.

Germany could learn more from progress made to ensure policies support development efforts of partner countries and communicate better on its efforts

Germany reports progress on policy coherence for development at the national and European levels. A section on progress in making policies development-friendly is included in the report that BMZ presents every four years to the Federal Parliament. The Federal Government's four-yearly progress report on the sustainable development strategy and the biennial indicator report prepared by the Statistical Office also help monitor progress. However, these reports are not frequent enough for sharing key examples of efforts to bring consistency across various German policies, such as its advocacy for phasing out EU export subsidies to agricultural products. Germany would gain from communicating its efforts and learning from their results more systematically. It is starting to do this, for example in its new partnership for sustainable textiles (see below). Commissioning and publishing independent reviews on a more regular basis could also strengthen the credibility of Germany's reporting.

Updating the national sustainable development strategy will offer opportunities to conduct forward-looking analysis and identify emerging areas of incoherence more systematically, drawing on the expertise of Germany's public research institutes, such as the German Development Institute (DIE) and the German Institute of Global and Area Studies (GIGA). Germany can also draw on the annual in-depth politico-economic analyses commissioned by BMZ as well as the political analyses that are conducted by German embassies in partner countries. These studies have the potential to identify areas involving competing interests. In a context where all embassy reporting goes to the Federal Foreign Office, it is important to ensure that relevant information is also shared with BMZ, the ministry responsible for policy coherence for development.[7]

Leading by example, Germany is driving the concept of decent work across supply chains

Germany prioritises sustainable development at home and worldwide. Noting that every person, as either consumer or employee, is integrated into international supply chains, Germany took the opportunity of its G7 Presidency in 2015 to advance the topic of decent work. It is encouraging G7 countries to take responsibility for implementing labour, social and environmental standards worldwide and to develop a G7 Supply Chain Initiative. Germany advocates for shared responsibilities and urges that all key stakeholders should be equipped to fulfil their proper responsibility (BMAS/BMZ, 2015).

Germany leads by example in promoting better standards. For instance, in 2015 it launched a Sustainable Standard Comparison Tool for improving transparency in the supply chain and helping consumers make more informed purchasing decisions. At the same time, Germany is enhancing its efforts to support responsible business along the supply chain. In particular, in October 2014 BMZ launched a partnership for sustainable textiles, in which German businesses, industry associations, trade unions and civil society representatives, and international sustainability initiatives and standards organisations come together to look at how to promote better standards and ensure they apply along the entire textile value chain (BMZ, 2014b). This partnership has grown from 35 to some 147 members (as of August 2015), accounting for a significant share of the German textile and garment market. While DEG (the German Investment and Development Corporation, a subsidiary of the German Government-owned development bank, KfW) has documented examples of how small changes can have a substantial impact at the level of individual companies,[8] joining forces beyond Germany is essential to give this initiative enough leverage and to avoid giving an unfair competitive advantage to companies which choose not to apply the same standards. Having made a start within its own country, Germany is taking a strategic approach by putting this agenda at the G7 as well as in the EU and the OECD.[9]

The German government also takes global sustainable development into account when promoting German exports. The ecological, social and development impacts are rigorously assessed when investigating whether an export transaction is eligible for official support. This is in line with OECD directives on officially supported export credits and environmental and social due diligence (OECD, 2012b). Germany also encourages the export of renewable energy technology as particularly eligible for export credit support.

Germany is doing well in implementing the OECD Anti-Bribery Convention, with many cases having been investigated. However, despite a change to the law, sanctions remain too low to be dissuasive and whistle blowers are not protected. The OECD report on Germany's implementation of the convention also notes that Germany needs to improve reporting on how it implements the convention by compiling statistics about sanctions automatically (OECD, 2013).

Financing for development

Indicator: The member engages in development finance in addition to ODA

Germany is actively engaged in leveraging private funds for sustainable development, with the technical and financial co-operation agencies GIZ and KfW using a wide range of tools. In particular, Germany promotes innovative mechanisms for climate finance, increasingly supports green investments in middle income countries and has efficient tools to foster responsible business growth.

Germany mobilises private sector development actions and capital

Consistent with its 2030 vision for sustainable development, Germany champions domestic resource mobilisation and good financial governance in partner countries while supporting private sector development and using official development assistance (ODA) as a catalyst to increase private financing. Germany helps partner countries in their efforts to increase domestic resources in various ways: i)strengthening national tax authorities in order to raise tax revenue; ii) improving fiscal transparency and budget management through supporting parliamentary budget committees, promoting financial systems development, deepening local capital markets (e.g. local currency bonds market development) and supporting activities such as the Extractive Industries Transparency Initiative; and iii) assisting decentralised authorities to generate local revenue.

Germany considers the private sector to be a key driver of development. Mobilising private financing for sustainable development is therefore a key component of Germany's development co-operation (Chapter 2). Strong links have been established with the German business community with a view to maximising private investment for sustainable development. Germany also seeks synergies among the public and private German actors in partner countries. In Mozambique, for example, BMZ has contributed to set up an office of the German Chamber of Commerce in Maputo to help leverage socially responsible business. In Kenya, the Head of the Delegation of German Industry and Commerce, the Head of Co-operation and Economy at the Embassy, and the Directors of KfW and GIZ (the two main development agencies), get together twice a year to exchange information and harmonise their approach to the private sector within the framework of Kenyan national priorities (Annex C).

Germany also stands out for its level of commitment to financing climate change activities in partner countries, and for its innovative approaches to financing. Germany's climate finance has quadrupled since 2005 to around EUR 2 billion in 2013. On average in 2011-13, Germany was the second highest provider of ODA to the environment as a whole after Japan (Chapter 2),[10] and was the first donor to make a pledge to the Green Climate Fund (of EUR 750 million in July 2014). Prior to this, Germany committed EUR 1.289 billion in climate finance under the Fast Start Finance period (2010-12), funding that was made available through BMZ and through the International Climate Initiative (Box 1.1).[11] At the G7 summit in May 2015, Chancellor Angela Merkel announced the aim to double Germany's international climate financing by 2020.

Box 1.1 Innovative mechanisms for climate finance

In BMZ and in the Federal Ministry for Environment, the Initiative for Climate and Environmental Protection (IKLU) and the International Climate Initiative (IKI) were created as innovative mechanisms funded through the sale of carbon market credits. BMZ and KfW committed between 2008 and 2013 EUR 8.9 billion through IKLU in the form of concessional loans for renewable energy, energy efficiency and low-energy transport in developing countries. Since 2015 this initiative is pursued under the heading "German Climate Technology Initiative" and also involves GIZ as an implementing partner. Since its creation in 2008 the International Climate Initiative has commissioned EUR 1.6 billion to climate and biodiversity projects in developing countries and emerging economies. It is a key element of Germany's climate and biodiversity financing portfolio, seeking to link with the international negotiations to support concrete actions and gain momentum. Initially set up as innovative mechanisms funded through the sale of carbon market credits, the initiatives are now funded through BMZ and the Ministry for Environment budgetary resources due to the declining revenues from the carbon credit market

Source: Data made available to the review team in Berlin; IKI website: http://www.international-climate-initiative.com.

Germany uses a wide range of tools to leverage private investment for sustainable development

Germany is at the forefront in using public development finance to leverage engagement and investment from the private sector for sustainable development. It mobilises a wide range of instruments and has developed some innovative approaches to engage with local, German and international companies. Its toolkit includes concessional loans, credit lines to local financial institutions, blended finance packages, public-private partnership arrangements, structured investment funds, risk capital provision, equity capital, mezzanine finance and guarantees.

As part of this, Germany increasingly supports green investments in middle-income countries such as the People's Republic of China, India and Turkey, where KfW provides loans and technical advice to local public and private banks to support environmentally friendly projects (e.g. on renewable energy). Long-term credit refinancing lines extended by KfW which target climate and environment protection enable banks to make financing available for investments by small and medium-sized companies.[12]

DEG, a subsidiary of KfW, is dedicated to promoting business initiatives in developing and emerging economies by financing operations and providing advisory services. By extending guarantees and equity and investing in high-risk tranches of development funds, it can attract investors from the private sector that would otherwise consider investment risks in developing countries too great for long-term engagement (Chapter 2). DEG also implements the Climate Partnerships with the Private Sector Programme. This programme, funded by the Ministry of Environment, invests in renewable and efficient energy for developing countries. DEG also seeks to foster responsible business growth through its investments. To ensure this, it has developed an evaluation tool to rate the performance of companies against a series of criteria (Box 1.2). As a result, DEG advises 60% of the companies it finances on implementation of environment and social standards, corporate governance, and corporate social responsibility. Germany also championed the establishment of a G20 dialogue platform for the mobilisation of institutional investor capital for green investment (GreenInvest) together with other partners.

Box 1.2 A rating tool for responsible business

In 2000 KfW/DEG introduced a corporate policy project rating that is mandatorily applied before any contract decision. This tool, further refined in 2002, measures the corporate and development quality of each investment in a transparent way during the entire project cycle. It comprises four benchmarks: i) the long-term profitability of the project; ii) its development impacts (e.g. in terms of job creation, tax revenue, gender impacts, technology transfer, compliance with social and environmental standards, etc.); iii) the additionality/leveraging role of DEG; and iv) the return of equity for DEG. The tool is also used ex-post for institutional learning and strategic management of the portfolio and for public relations. This tool has become a market standard and is now used as a steering and evaluation instrument by 15 development finance institutions and funds around the world.

Source: KfW/DEG (2013), Corporate-Policy Project Rating – Brief Description (May 2013)

Germany reports non-ODA flows appropriately

Germany tracks and reports the totality of its resource flows (not only ODA) to developing countries. These include:

- part of the loans extended by KfW (USD 313 million in gross disbursements in 2013) and DEG's loans (USD 911 million), which are both categorised as other official flows;
- Euler-Hermes' (Germany's official export credit agency) export credits (USD 12.7 billion in 2013 in gross disbursements), which mostly correspond to officially-guaranteed export credits and – to a lesser extent – to official direct export credits;[13]
- foreign direct investment (USD 11.2 billion in 2013 in net disbursements), private bonds and other securities (USD 11.8 billion), which are all categorised as private flows at market terms;
- private charitable flows (USD 1.4 billion in 2013), which correspond to the grants from the German non-government sector (i.e. NGOs and foundations).

As regards climate policy objectives, Germany is one of the few DAC members reporting its other official flows against the Rio marker on climate change. However, this reporting is not yet complete. It covers only the KfW Development Bank and not DEG. This is because Germany lacks the information systems needed to track this.

Notes

1. German priorities for the G7 Summit in Schloss Elmau on 7-8 June 2015 were: the post-2015 agenda; decent working conditions; protecting the climate; strengthening health care systems; strengthening women economically; food security; the CONNEX Initiative, which aims to assist developing countries in complex contract negotiations; the Deauville Partnership; accountability; dialogue with Africa; and civil society.

2. For instance, in the OECD, Germany advocated for making policy coherence for development a thematic focus of the OECD Strategy for Development (OECD, 2012a).

3. The German Government's 14th development policy White Paper also states that development policy will be co-ordinated with other policy areas, making an important contribution to policy coherence for development (BMZ, 2013).

4. In doing so, Germany could look at the Commitment to Development Index produced by the Center for Global Development. Germany ranked 12th out of 27 countries in 2014, with positive results for international trade, migration, research and investment. According to the Center, Germany could increase its ranking by increasing its aid budget, decreasing its greenhouse gas emissions, promoting financial transparency and participating in international peacekeeping efforts (CGD, 2015). These are all areas in which Germany is making progress.

5. The report highlights the following as good practices: Germany's water-land-energy nexus approach that takes into consideration the mutual impact of energy, water and food security policies; its efforts to ensure coherence between its legal migration policy and development objectives; and its socially and environmentally responsible approach to biofuel production.

6. The 2014 Federal budget stipulates that BMZ "seeks to ensure policy coherence for development within the German government and the European Union" (Federal Government, 2013).

7. Although the main addressee is the Federal Foreign Office, reports by German embassies can be copied directly to the other ministries concerned.

8. For instance the DBL Group, a Bangladeshi garment manufacturer, has managed to improve the working and safety standard in its factories while remaining competitive.

9. BMZ is chairing the OECD Advisory Group on Responsible Supply Chains in the Textile and Garment Sector.

10. On average in 2011-13, Germany was the top DAC provider to biodiversity, the second highest to combatting climate change (having committed USD 2.7 billion to climate change mitigation and USD 1.8 billion to climate change adaptation), and the third to desertification (OECD DAC Creditor Reporting System, 2014).

11. More details in Chapter 6 of Germany's 6th National Communication to the United Nations Framework Convention on Climate Change and Chapter 5 of Germany's First Biennial Report to the UNFCCC (BMUB, 2013 and Federal Republic of Germany, 2014).

12. For example, KfW made available a credit line of EUR 50 million to India's National Housing Bank, which offers home loans for energy-efficient buildings; it provided the Export-Import-Bank of China with a loan of EUR 75 million to support the establishment of two credit lines to finance the development of renewable energy sources and modern technologies for improved energy efficiency; a loan to Turkey's Seberbank helped it to launch the first private loan scheme for financing environmentally friendly projects.

13. Officially-guaranteed or insured export credits are categorised as private flows at market terms while official direct export credits are categorised as other official flows.

Bibliography

Government sources

BMAS/BMZ (2015), *Good Work Worldwide – Vision Paper*, February 2015, *Braunschweigische Maschinenbauanstalt AG* and *Bundesministerium für wirtschaftliche Zusammenarbeit und Entwicklung* Berlin, available at: www.bmz.de/en/publications/type_of_publication/information_flyer/information_brochures/Materialie241_lieferketten.pdf.

BMUB (2013), *Sixth National Communication under the United Nations Framework on Climate Change – Report by the German Federal Government,* December 2013, *Bundesministeriums für Umwelt, Naturschutz, Bau und Reaktorsicherheit,* Berlin, available at: http://unfccc.int/files/national_reports/annex_i_natcom/submitted_natcom/application/pdf/national_communication_eng_bf.pdf.

BMZ (2014a), *Charter for the Future - One World, Our Responsibility*, BMZ, Bonn.

BMZ (2014b), *Sustainable Textiles: What German development policy is doing*, BMZ, Bonn, available at www.bmz.de/en/publications/topics/health/Materialie240_textilbuendnis.pdf.

BMZ (2013), *The German Government 14th Development Policy Report – Development Policy White Paper*, May 2013, BMZ, Bonn.

CDU/CSU/SPD (2014), "Responsibility in the world", Chapter 7 in *Shaping Germany's Future – Coalition treaty between CDU/CSU and SPD – 18th legislative period*, Berlin, unofficial translation, available at: www.kas.de/wf/doc/kas_36853-544-2-30.pdf?140820093605.

Federal Government (2014), *Post-2015 Agenda for Sustainable Development - Key positions of the German government*, February 2014, Berlin, https://sustainabledevelopment.un.org/content/documents/8778germany.pdf.

Federal Government (2013), *Federal Budget 2014, Departmental Budget 23,* Federal Ministry for Economic Co-operation and Development, Berlin.

Federal Government (2012a), *National Sustainable Development Strategy, Progress Report 2012*, February 2012, Berlin, available at: www.bundesregierung.de/Content/DE/_Anlagen/Nachhaltigkeit-wiederhergestellt/2012-06-07-fortschrittsbericht-2012-englisch-barrierefrei.pdf?__blob=publicationFile.

Federal Government (2012b), *10 Years of Sustainability "made in Germany" – National Sustainable Development Strategy*, April 2012, Berlin.

Federal Republic of Germany (2014), *First Biennial Report by the Federal Republic of Germany Pursuant to Decision 1/CP.16, April 2013,* Report under the United Nations Framework Convention on Climate Change, available at: http://unfccc.int/files/national_reports/annex_i_natcom/submitted_natcom/application/pdf/141022_br_2014_germany_english.resubmission.pdf.

FFO (2012), *Shaping Globalization – Expanding Partnerships – Sharing Responsibility, A Strategy Paper by the German Government*, Federal Foreign Office, Berlin, available at: www.auswaertiges-amt.de/cae/servlet/contentblob/616584/publicationFile/190244/Gestaltungsmaechtekonzept%20engl.pdf.

KfW (2014), *Sustainability Guidelines, Evaluation of Environmental, Social, and Climate Aspects: Principles and Process*, KfW Development Bank, Frankfurt, available at: www.kfw-entwicklungsbank.de/PDF/Download-Center/PDF-Dokumente-Richtlinien/Nachhaltigkeitsrichtlinie_EN.pdf.

KfW/DEG (2013), *Corporate-Policy Project Rating – Brief Description*, KfW/DEG, Frankfurt.

Other sources

CGD (2015), *Commitment to Development Index 2014*, Center for Global Development, Washington, DC, available at: www.cgdev.org/sites/default/files/commitment-development-index-print.pdf.

EC (2013), *EU 2013 Report on Policy Coherence for Development*, 31 October 2013, European Commission, Brussels, available at: https://ec.europa.eu/europeaid/sites/devco/files/pcd-report-2013_en.pdf.

OECD (2014), *OECD Economic Surveys: Germany 2014*, OECD Publishing, Paris, http://dx.doi.org/10.1787/eco_surveys-deu-2014-en.

OECD (2013), *Germany: Follow-up to the Phase 3 Report and Recommendations*, April 2013, Paris, available at: www.oecd.org/daf/anti-bribery/GermanyPhase3WrittenFollowUpEN.pdf.

OECD (2012a), *OECD Strategy on Development*, Paris, http://www.oecd.org/pcd/OECD%20Development%20Strategy.pdf.

OECD (2012b), *Recommendation of the Council on Common Approaches for Officially Supported Export Credits and Environmental and Social Due Diligence (the "common approaches")*, June 2012, Paris, available at: www.agaportal.de/pdf/nachhaltigkeit/info/e_common_approaches.pdf.

Chapter 2: Germany's vision and policies for development co-operation

Policies, strategies and commitments

Indicator: Clear policy vision and solid strategies guide the programme

Germany has established an overarching, value-driven policy for development co-operation, which seeks to advance sustainable development as both a domestic and global issue. BMZ now needs to translate the widely-owned vision into an operational framework that integrates the new ministerial priorities and helps work better across government, in order to inform programming and guide partners.

Germany's agenda for sustainable development is widely-owned

Since December 2013, the Coalition Treaty *Shaping Germany's Future* has been guiding Germany's policy for development co-operation, outlining its objectives and values (CDU/CSU/SPD, 2014). The Charter for the Future, published by BMZ in November 2014 following broad consultation, builds on the treaty to provide a comprehensive vision for German development policy (BMZ, 2014a). This charter aims to bring together as many stakeholders as possible to make a broad-based, country-owned contribution to sustainable development, at home and abroad. With its eight priority areas, this transformative agenda provides a useful platform for dialogue with various stakeholders and society as a whole, and as such is conducive to a widely-owned approach to the 2030 Agenda. The charter adds to the objectives set in the Coalition Treaty two operational priorities on promoting innovation and partnerships. Finally, three special initiatives launched by the Minister for Development Co-operation in 2014 address pressing needs and come on top of the other priorities (Table 2.1).

Table 2.1 German development co-operation: purpose and strategic vision

Objectives of the Coalition Treaty (2013)	Priority areas in the Charter for the Future (2014)
1) Defeat hunger and poverty 2) Strengthen democracy and the rule of law 3) Advocate for peace, freedom and security 4) Advocate respect for and observance of human rights 5) Protect the environment 6) Encourage a socially and ecologically oriented market economy 7) Promote good governance, and strengthen participation by civil society	1) Ensure a life of dignity for all everywhere 2) Protect natural resources and manage them sustainably 3) Combine economic growth, sustainability and decent work 4) Promote and ensure human rights and good governance 5) Build peace and strengthen human security 6) Respect and protect cultural and religious diversity 7) Drive transformational change through innovation, technology and digitalisation 8) Forge a new global partnership and develop multi-stakeholder partnerships for sustainable development.
Three special initiatives (2014)	
1) One world – no hunger; 2) Fighting the root causes of displacement, reintegrating refugees; and 3) Stability and development in the Middle East and North Africa region.	

Source: Coalition Treaty (CDU/CSU/SPD, 2014), Charter for the Future (BMZ, 2014a) *and memorandum* (BMZ, 2015).

While the charter provides a broad basis for development co-operation, a useful next step would be to support its implementation with strategic messages to provide guidance and predictability for partners; such guidance will help to clarify the hierarchy of priorities, including the three special initiatives launched in 2014. In doing so, Germany should build on the new strategic framework it began developing in 2013.[1]

Looking forward, given that the SDGs will be universal in application and will require non-ODA finance in addition to traditional co-operation, BMZ will need to be able to play an integral part in whole-of-government policy processes with respect to both international development and sustainable development in the domestic arena (Chapters 1 and 4). In addressing sustainable development at home and abroad, the Charter provides BMZ with a useful entry point to promote cross-government approaches.

Approach to allocating bilateral and multilateral aid

Indicator: The rationale for allocating aid and other resources is clear and evidence-based

BMZ's allocations are context-based and target poor countries. Germany's strategic engagement with multilateral organisations and its intention to use multilateral and bilateral instruments in a flexible way according to their comparative advantages will help increase the development programme's impact by selecting the most effective channel for each context. However, having distinct budget lines for different actors with amounts not closely related to the programme needs makes it more difficult to tailor the mix of instruments to each situation and build synergies within the bilateral programme.

Bilateral allocations and instruments are context-based and focus on reducing poverty, but budgetary mechanisms bring rigidity in programming

Germany's policy is focused on the poorest countries, in particular in Africa. It is striving to concentrate its programme further by offering a full bilateral programme to fewer partner countries (down from 57 in 2010 to 50), while maintaining less in-depth co-operation in a further 29 countries (Chapter 3). A set of regional quotas and sector/thematic spending targets guide country allocation decisions. These decisions are made annually on the basis of the funding allocated by parliament to technical co-operation and financial co-operation respectively. BMZ uses a "Catalogue of Criteria" to assess the development orientation of partner countries in terms of: i) pro-poor and sustainable policy design; ii) respecting, protecting and guaranteeing all human rights, democracy and the rule of law; iii) State effectiveness and transparency; and iv) co-operative behaviour within the international community. While these criteria are meant, among other tools, to help BMZ decide whether and in what form Germany engages in development co-operation with a particular country, arbitrations are made in a flexible way and in relation with the country strategy units at headquarters and staff working on development co-operation in embassies. With Germany indicating a further focus on fragile countries, the "Catalogue of Criteria", which emphasises partner countries' good governance and effectiveness as criteria for engagement, should be revisited if it is to remain relevant as a tool for directing German ODA allocations.

If not dealt with carefully, a number of budgetary mechanisms may be undermining the effectiveness of the German programme. Fixed and separate allocations for technical co-operation and financial co-operation make the system somewhat disconnected from the needs of the programme, an obstacle that GIZ and KfW are trying to overcome pragmatically (Chapter 5). Separate budget lines also exist for six political foundations and the development associations of two major Churches (Protestant and Catholic). This system allows these actors to engage in countries or sectors that are not eligible for the bilateral programme. Better co-ordination with BMZ would increase the potential for maximising synergies with the development programme. Funding allocation decisions for the special initiatives launched in 2014 also follow a different logic and process. While they reflect a high level political commitment and provide more flexibility, experience shows that this makes the programming process more complex at country level (Chapter 5).

Within country programmes, decisions on thematic and sector allocations as well as instruments are context-based, relying on suggestions made by the BMZ country units in conjunction with GIZ and KfW. While low-income countries usually receive grants, projects that are economically viable and make a significant contribution to domestic growth may be funded through loans, provided the country's debt is manageable. In Kenya, for example, Germany uses a variety of instruments within a clear framework for providing grants and concessional loans for activities targeting poverty in middle-income countries. This shows that those who have a stake in German development co-operation are able to co-ordinate their approach and agree on which instruments are suited for each context. In differentiating development co-operation approaches according to the characteristics of partner countries, Germany is well positioned for the future, since context-based approaches will become more important to deal effectively with a broader agenda.

Germany is engaging more strategically with multilateral organisations

Before 2013, the allocation of Germany's ODA was set at two-thirds for bilateral aid and one-third for multilateral aid in accordance with a binding decision of the Budgetary Committee of the German Parliament. This cap on multilateral aid was also stipulated in the Federal Government's 2009 coalition agreement. In December 2013, the new coalition agreement stated that bilateral and multilateral instruments could be used in a flexible way according to their comparative advantages, thereby abolishing the cap. It also decreed that contributions to multilateral development organisations could be decided according to their effectiveness and performance.

In this context, in 2014 BMZ commissioned a study of its co-operation with 30 multilateral organisations and vertical funds. Using existing information from the organisations themselves and the Multilateral Organisation Performance Assessment Network (MOPAN) - a good practice encouraged by the DAC - the study assesses their performance against the following criteria: mandate, relevance, performance and opportunities for strategic co-operation with BMZ. The findings will primarily serve as a basis for driving reforms of international organisations. In some cases, they may also lead to reviewing resource allocations.

Following a recommendation in the 2010 peer review (OECD, 2011 and Annex A), Germany has taken steps to engage strategically with multilateral organisations, for which it has developed "Guiding Principles for Multilateral Development Policy" (BMZ, 2014b). Germany is an active player in the reform process of the multilateral system, engaging constructively on governing boards to help multilateral organisations fulfil their mandates more effectively. In recent years, Germany has proactively helped to advance various processes, including the Joint Programming Initiative of the European Union and its Member States, the UN institutions' Delivering as One initiative and the reform of the World Bank's trust fund activities. BMZ is also active in various fora for reducing earmarked contributions to multilateral organisations and improving the quality and management of this type of financing. Germany also plays an active role, in collaboration with the OECD, in the Senior Level Donor Meeting on Multilateral Reform.

In its approach to climate change, Germany ensures co-ordination and consistency across the various ministries involved in allocating core and non-core resources to multilateral organisations. Germany should build on this to ensure that a co-ordinated approach to the multilateral system becomes systematic across government.

Policy focus

Indicator: Fighting poverty, especially in least developed countries and fragile states, is prioritised

Germany aims to reduce poverty and promotes development underpinned by democracy and good governance, social and environmental responsibility and a market-based economy. A strong policy framework supports engagement in fragile contexts, but Germany should strengthen links between humanitarian and development programming. Germany prioritises environment and climate change and is taking serious steps to address gender equality. Assigning champions for advocacy and allocating adequate resources would help to implement selected cross-cutting issues effectively.

Germany's development policy is clearly focused on reducing poverty and promoting democracy, good governance and a market orientation

The poverty focus of Germany's development co-operation is apparent to all German stakeholders, at headquarters and in partner countries, underpinned by clear statements and solid guidance. The 2013 Coalition Treaty sets reducing hunger and poverty and strengthening democracy and the rule of law as the primary objective of development co-operation. BMZ has a cross-sectoral strategy that puts reducing poverty at the core of development co-operation, and GIZ and KfW explicitly refer to this strategy in their programming guidance (BMZ, 2012). Reducing poverty is dealt with as a cross-cutting issue, with a multi-dimensional approach and close links to building capacity.

The Coalition Treaty also outlines Germany's readiness to contribute to crisis and conflict resolution, and its support for prevention as well as conflict and post-conflict management, with a particular focus on fragile states (CDU/CSU/SPD, 2014). In line with this emphasis, Parliament now has a subcommittee on conflict resolution, and the new special initiatives support programmes that are related to fragility.

Germany's policy framework for development co-operation is in line with international goals and priorities. It emphasises good governance as a prerequisite for sustainable development, focusing specifically on financial governance, including taxation and domestic resource mobilisation. This focus applies both to the bilateral programme and to multilateral engagement. As an illustration, Germany led the global dialogue on strengthening capacities and building effective institutions during the post-2015 consultations. Germany also hosts the International Tax Compact platform that aims to promote effective, fair and transparent tax systems. It also champions domestic resource mobilisation in the DAC network on governance and in the Effective Institutions Platform.

Germany also considers a market economy to be of key importance for achieving sustainable development. Engaging with the private sector is a long-standing feature of Germany's development co-operation. Recognising this feature, the 2010 peer review recommended that Germany develop its private sector programme to encourage foreign and domestic investments in areas aligned to partner countries' development strategies, while ensuring that this does not divert ODA to finance assistance that is oriented to its own commercial interests. Germany has multiple entry points in place to promote private investment, as shown in the infrastructure sector (Figure 2.1). This enables it to cover a very wide spectrum of activities, while also using innovative instruments, developing synergies between different actors and adapting the mix of instruments to national contexts (Chapter 1). While Germany focuses on areas where it can add specific value (e.g. renewable energy), its support is aligned to partner country priorities, and international tendering procedures ensure aid is untied (Chapter 5).

Figure 2.1 How Germany promotes private infrastructure investment in developing countries

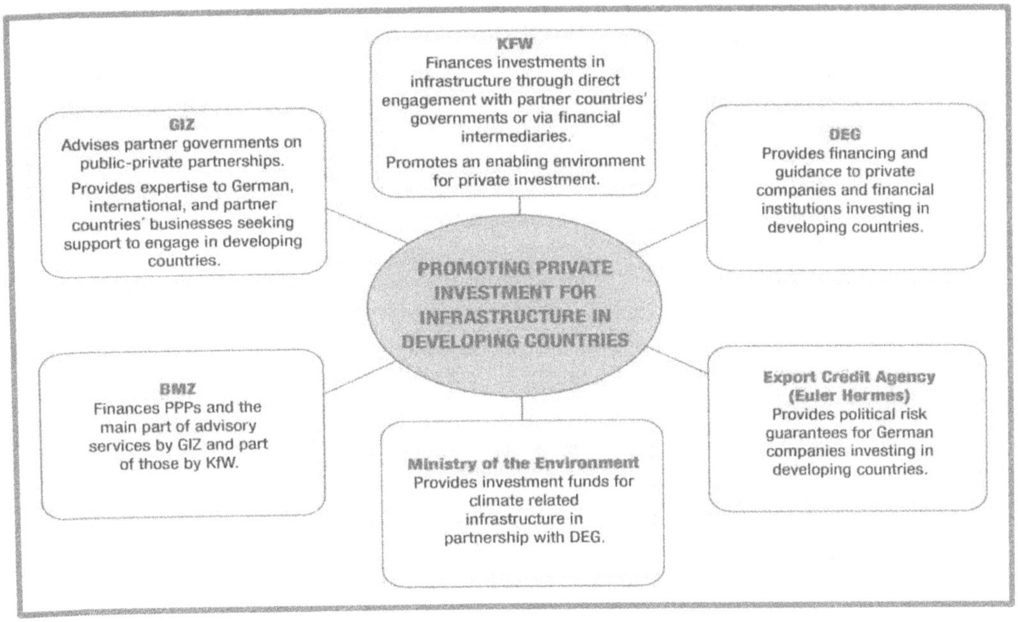

Source: Miyamoto, K. and K. Biousse (2014), Development Co-operation Working Papers, No. 19, "Official Support for Private Sector Participation in Developing Country Infrastructure".

Links between humanitarian and development programming could be clearer

The 2010 peer review found that links between humanitarian and development programming were unclear, a finding echoed by an evaluation of German humanitarian aid conducted jointly by BMZ and the Federal Foreign Office in 2012 (BMZ/FFO, 2012). There is still a lack of clarity over BMZ's tools for transitional assistance and the special initiatives, limiting Germany's ability to support holistic responses systematically in protracted crises and recovery situations (Chapter 7). Germany is encouraged to make clear its approach towards transition programming.

A strong policy framework supports engagement in fragile contexts

There are new inter-ministerial guidelines for working in fragile contexts (FFO/MOD/BMZ, 2013) complemented by a BMZ strategy paper on development for peace and security (BMZ, 2013). These meet a recommendation made in the 2010 peer review. The inter-ministerial guidelines are built on international good practice and set out the core tasks that are essential in fragile contexts. They also include medium and long-term peacebuilding and statebuilding objectives, as well as crisis prevention – and clearly recognise the need for long-term engagement. The Fragile States Principles and the New Deal are incorporated, and the role of the UN and regional organisations in providing legitimacy is highlighted. BMZ's strategy paper complements these guidelines, taking a conflict-sensitive approach and aiming to contribute to the peacebuilding and statebuilding goals. Helpfully, different types of programmes are identified that match classifications of fragility based on various mixes of state capacity, authority and legitimacy. It is not clear, however, how the special initiatives link to fragile states policy, or how they incorporate key fragility concepts such as conflict sensitivity and "do no harm" (Chapter 5).

Germany prioritises environment and climate change and is taking serious steps to address gender inequality

Climate change is increasingly a core priority for Germany. Along with environment and natural resources issues, climate change is well embedded in the programme, both thematically and as a cross-cutting dimension. Since 2010, more than 40% of Germany's bilateral ODA commitments have targeted activities related to climate change and the environment – almost double the average for all OECD DAC members.[2] About one-third of GIZ's projects were related to climate change in 2013, and 64% of all new commitments by KfW in 2014 were for climate and environmental financing.

Germany supports activities in the areas of biodiversity, climate change, desertification and green growth. It helps partner countries to identify the causes of environmental and climate risks, strengthen their governance structures and policies, and develop regional co-operation. Capacity building and technology transfer are key components of Germany's support.[3] Germany also uses official development finance to leverage engagement and investment from the private sector (Chapter 1).

BMZ introduced an Environmental and Climate Assessment Tool in 2011 to help mainstream environment and climate issues across all of its development co-operation portfolio. It is used systematically to: i) embed environmental and climate protection and adaptation as cross-cutting topics in sector and country strategies; and ii) reduce or avoid negative environmental and climate impacts, and increase environmental and climate potential benefits of all programmes implemented by the German implementing agencies. In line with this tool, all bilateral projects are screened at the appraisal phase. Results of the screening are reviewed by BMZ country divisions. On top of this screening, the sector divisions on climate and environment reviewed in 2014 about half of bilateral programme proposals. This process has an impact since, on average, one out of two screened proposals underwent adjustments or were given specific comments for implementation.[4]

Germany's use and quality control of the OECD DAC's environmental policy markers are rigorous.[5] This is illustrated by KfW's internal guidance for applying the climate markers, which includes sectoral examples; and by BMZ's system for tracking the biodiversity components of projects.[6] Germany is actively involved in a number of international climate initiatives and in the OECD work on environment and climate change, including co-chairing the DAC-EPOC Task Team on Climate Change and Development.[7] It could do more to share its expertise and experience on environment and development co-operation with the DAC.

BMZ also takes steps to integrate gender equality into its programme through a comprehensive three-pronged approach of political dialogue, empowerment and gender mainstreaming (BMZ, 2014c) and a screening mechanism. In 2013, 42% of German bilateral sector allocable aid had gender equality and women's empowerment as a principal or significant objective, compared with a DAC country average of 33%. GIZ and KfW have gender experts and focal points on gender equality within departments at headquarters and country offices (for GIZ). Meanwhile BMZ has only 1.3 full-time equivalent staff dedicated to this issue. While it relies on the gender expertise located within the implementing agencies, lack of internal resources hinders BMZ's ability to oversee the agencies and to learn from good practice.

BMZ should clarify how to deal with other cross-cutting issues.[8] Recognising that it is hard to follow-up effectively on many cross-cutting issues in parallel, German country teams in partner countries prioritise specific cross-cutting issues depending on context. For example, in Kenya there is a specific focus on anti-corruption while, in Mozambique, the health situation has led Germany to focus on HIV/AIDs. This seems a pragmatic approach provided choice of focus is backed by solid, context-specific analysis. Meanwhile assigning advocacy champions at senior levels of the organisation and allocating adequate resources would facilitate effective implementation across all sectors as well as in policy dialogue. This is particularly relevant for gender equality, at a time when BMZ is developing an action plan to implement its 2014 cross-sectoral gender strategy. A high-level commitment to prioritising gender equality and making it mandatory to embed gender equality results into core reporting frameworks could boost progress already made.

Notes

1. Since 2013, BMZ has been producing strategy papers on energy, urbanisation, gender equality, good financial governance, civil society organisations, multilateral organisation, the private sector, and fragile states.

2. Source: OECD DAC Creditor Reporting System, 12 December 2014.

3. For example, GIZ has been active in building the capacity of small and medium-sized cities to reduce air pollution and the carbon intensity of travel. Germany also supports partner countries to co-operate regionally on environmental issues and supports tools and strategies to integrate environmental protection into other policy areas, e.g. through capacity building to perform Strategic Environmental Assessments. Between 2005 and 2013, GIZ also helped to set up the Renewable Energy Policy Network for the 21st Century (REN21) (on behalf of BMZ and the Ministry of Environment) to support knowledge sharing, policy development and joint action to achieve a rapid global transition to renewable energy.

4. KfW has an overarching environmental, climate change and social impact assessment policy, the adherence to which is monitored closely by a central policy unit, the "competence centre environment and climate". Every three years KfW publishes a sustainability report that brings together the results of its policy (KfW, 2014).

5. There is systematic quality review of the application of the Rio markers by sector experts, statistical units conduct regular coverage and consistency checks, and training and awareness-raising is conducted for officers in charge of marking.

6. Under this system, introduced in 2012, the volume of the specific biodiversity "sectoral component" of a project is identified, and only this volume is calculated as a contribution towards biodiversity conservation, rather than the value of the whole project. BMZ is now preparing a guidance for applying the climate markers.

7. As a member of the task team on improving the Rio markers, environment and development finance statistics, GIZ took part in the Stocktake of OECD DAC Members' Reporting Practices on Environment-related Official Development Finance and Reporting to the Rio Conventions in December 2013. Germany also hosted the second meeting of the Joint ENVIRONET-WP-STAT Task Team in Bonn in June 2014.

8. BMZ has four cross-cutting issues: poverty reduction; good governance and anti-corruption; human rights and gender equality; and climate change and the environment.

Bibliography

Government sources

BMZ (2015), *OECD DAC Peer Review of Germany 2015 – Memorandum by Germany, BMZ,* Bonn.

BMZ (2014a), *Charter for the Future - One world, Our Responsibility*, BMZ, Bonn.

BMZ (2014b), "Guiding principles for multilateral development policy", BMZ Strategy Paper 7/2013e, BMZ, Bonn, available at: www.bmz.de/en/publications/type_of_publication/strategies/Strategiepapier336_07_2013.pdf.

BMZ (2014c), "Gender equality in German development policy - Cross-sectoral strategy", BMZ Strategy Paper 2/2014e, BMZ, Bonn, available at: www.bmz.de/en/publications/type_of_publication/strategies/Strategiepapier340_02_2014.pdf.

BMZ (2012), "Fighting poverty more effectively – worldwide – cross-sectoral strategy on poverty reduction", BMZ Strategy Paper 6/2012e, BMZ, Bonn, available at: www.bmz.de/en/publications/type_of_publication/strategies/Strategiepapier325_06_2012.pdf.

BMZ (2009), "Promotion of good governance in German development policy", Strategies 178, February 2009, BMZ, Bonn, available at: www.bmz.de/en/publications/type_of_publication/strategies/konzept178.pdf.

BMZ (2007), "Development-oriented transformation in conditions of fragile statehood and poor government performance", Strategies 153, BMZ, Bonn, available at: www.oecd.org/dacfragilestates/43480415.pdf.

CDU/CSU/SPD (2014), "Responsibility in the world", Chapter 7 in *Shaping Germany's Future – Coalition treaty between CDU/CSU and SPD – 18th legislative period*, Berlin, unofficial translation, available at: www.kas.de/wf/doc/kas_36853-544-2-30.pdf?140820093605.

GIZ (2012), *Gender Pays Off: GIZ Gender Strategy, Deutsche Gesellschaft für Internationale Zusammenarbeit*, Bonn, available at: www.giz.de/expertise/downloads/Fachexpertise/giz-gender-strategy-en-2012.pdf.

KfW (2014), *Sustainability guidelines, Evaluation of Environmental, Social, and Climate Aspects: Principles and Process,* KFW Development Bank, Frankfurt, available at: www.kfw-entwicklungsbank.de/PDF/Download-Center/PDF-Dokumente-Richtlinien/Nachhaltigkeitsrichtlinie_EN.pdf.

KfW (2011), *The Gender Strategy of KfW Development Bank*, September 2011, KfW Development Bank, Frankfurt, available at: www.kfw-entwicklungsbank.de/Download-Center/PDF-Dokumente-Selbstdarstellung/2011_Genderstrategie_E.pdf.

Other sources

Miyamoto, K. and K. Biousse (2014), "Official Support for Private Sector Participation in Developing Country Infrastructure", *OECD Development Co-operation Working Papers*, No. 19, OECD Publishing, Paris. DOI: http://dx.doi.org/10.1787/5jz14cd40nf0-en

OECD (2011), *OECD Development Assistance Peer Reviews: Germany 2010*, OECD Publishing, Paris, available at: http://dx.doi.org/10.1787/9789264098299-en.

Chapter 3: Allocating Germany's official development assistance

Overall ODA volume

Indicator: The member makes every effort to meet ODA domestic and international targets

The German government has reaffirmed its commitment to meet the UN target of allocating 0.7% of its gross national income (GNI) as ODA and has announced important increases in its aid budget between 2014 and 2019. In 2014, German net ODA reached a historic high, bringing the ODA/GNI ratio from 0.38% to 0.41%. However, in light of Germany's economic growth, further planned increases will only be sufficient to maintain ODA at a minimum level of 0.4% as a percentage of GNI, far from the 0.7% target. Germany has yet to adopt a timeline for meeting its ODA/GNI commitment.

Important increases in ODA are planned

In 2014, Germany provided USD 16.25 billion in net ODA, a 12% increase in real terms from 2013 (preliminary figures). This increase brought the country's net ODA to GNI ratio to 0.41% in 2014, up from 0.35% in 2009 (Figure 3.1). Germany is the third largest DAC donor in terms of volume and the tenth in terms of its net ODA as a percentage of GNI.[1]

Germany has reaffirmed its commitment to meeting the UN 0.7% ODA/GNI target and has announced important further increases in aid volumes. The 2013 Coalition Treaty committed the new government to provide EUR 2 billion in extra aid during the legislative period through to 2017 (BMZ, 2015a). Most recently, the German Cabinet announced an additional increase in the aid budget of EUR 8.3 billion between 2015 and 2019.[2] According to projections by the German government, a large part of this additional funding will benefit BMZ, bringing its budget from EUR 6.5 billion in 2015 to EUR 7.5 billion in 2017, its highest level ever.[3] The Federal Foreign Office (for humanitarian assistance) and the Ministry of Environment will also receive additional funding.

Figure 3.1 Germany's net ODA by volume and as a share of gross national income, 1998-2014

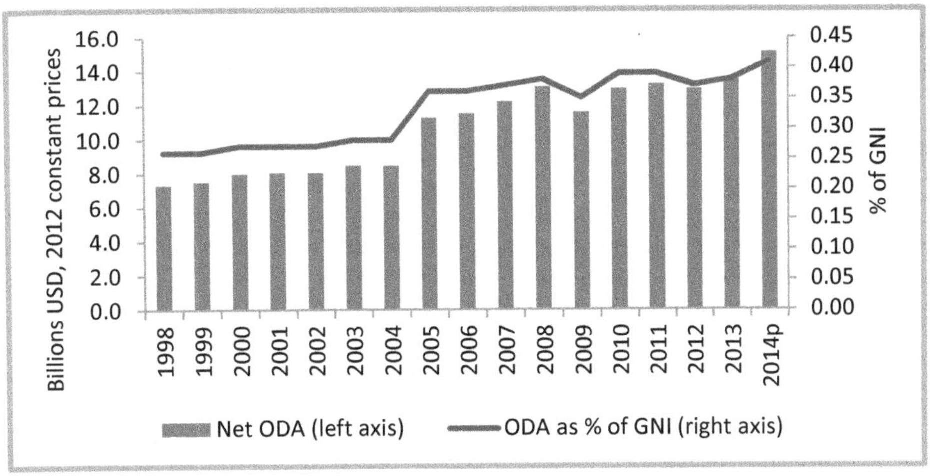

Source: DAC statistics

Germany needs a plan and timeline for achieving the 0.7% ODA/GNI target

The additional amount of EUR 10.3 billion being made available for development co-operation between 2014 and 2019 shows that Germany is determined to increase spending quite significantly in the next few years, with the objective of maintaining its ODA/GNI ratio at a level of at least 0.40%. However, despite these important increases in ODA, the 0.7% target is still a long way off and the government has not defined a timeframe or intermediate targets for achieving it, as was recommended in the 2010 peer review (Annex A).[4] Such a plan could usefully outline how Germany will spend additional funding, including through special initiatives (Chapter 2).

Germany could take advantage of its growing ODA envelope to scale up its support to least developed countries (LDCs) and fragile states. In a context where Germany's total ODA to LDCs as a share of GNI was 0.09% in 2013, well below the UN target of 0.15% (OECD, 2015b), an increase of ODA to countries most in need would be in line with the commitment made at the DAC high-level meeting in December 2014 (OECD, 2014b).

Germany complies with DAC reporting guidelines and recommendations

Germany complies with DAC reporting guidelines, providing timely, complete, accurate and good quality information. Germany also reports indicative expenditures for the coming three years, aggregated for all government departments, to the DAC Indicative Forward Spending Survey (OECD, 2014a).

ODA loans are a major feature of German development co-operation. The share of loans in Germany's gross bilateral ODA disbursements increased from 19% in 2009 to 26% in 2013. The grant element of Germany's total ODA commitments fell to 86.9% in 2013, from 88.4% in 2012 and 97.5% in 2002-03. This still complies with the OECD Recommendation on aid terms and conditions, which requires a grant element of at least 86%.[5]

Bilateral ODA allocations

Indicator: Aid is allocated according to the statement of intent and international commitments

Bilateral ODA allocations reflect only partially Germany's political commitment to focus on the poorest countries, especially in Africa. Germany has reduced the number of partner countries to 50, but this has not increased ODA concentration. KfW uses a range of less concessional financing instruments targeting higher-income developing countries, a fact which explains the discrepancies between political intentions and actual spending. While using different tools in different contexts is positive, Germany's share of bilateral ODA allocated to the least developed and other low-income countries is decreasing. Sector allocations, however, do reflect Germany's policy focus on poverty reduction, governance, economic growth and environment.

Fewer partner countries has not led to greater concentration of ODA

Germany's share of bilateral ODA has increased in recent years, reaching 71% of its total gross ODA in 2013, up from 63% in 2009 (Table B.2, Annex B). Following a recommendation in the 2010 peer review (Annex A), Germany decided to further concentrate its bilateral aid on 50 partner countries,[6] down from 92 in 2005 and 57 in 2010 (BMZ, 2015a). Despite this stronger focus, aid concentration has decreased since 2002: the top 20 countries received 47% of German bilateral ODA on average between 2007 and 2011, but only 43% in 2012-13 (Table B.4). This trend can be accounted for by an increase in funds which are unallocated geographically or allocated only regionally, reflecting Germany's increased focus on regional programmes and initiatives. In addition, four of Germany's top ten beneficiaries are not on the list of 50 partner countries with a full bilateral programme (China, Côte d'Ivoire, Syria and Turkey) (Table B.4).

Germany's share of country programmable aid has remained quite stable over the past four years, reaching 52% of bilateral ODA in 2013 (Figure 3.2), just below the DAC country average of 54.5%.[7] This means that nearly half of German bilateral aid is not available for programming at partner country level: 22% of bilateral aid is unallocated, including funds to political foundations and the two main church-based organisations, while imputed student costs, humanitarian aid, debt relief and administrative costs combined account for 24% of bilateral aid.

Figure 3.2 Composition of Germany's bilateral ODA, 2013 gross disbursements

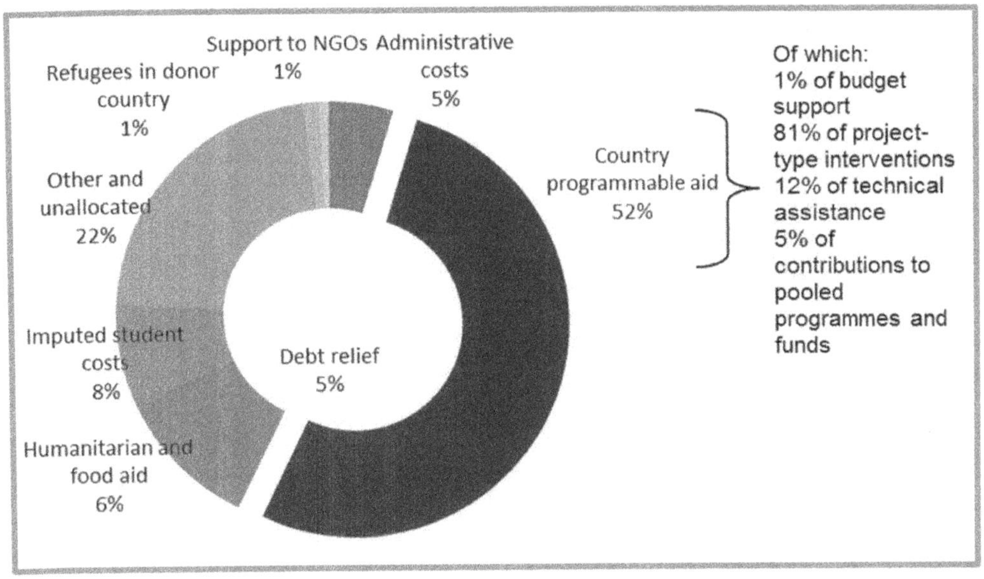

Source: DAC statistics

Loans to middle-income countries dilute Germany's bilateral ODA focus on the poorest countries

In line with the commitment to focus on the poorest countries, BMZ is prioritising Africa as a region. From 2015 it plans to allocate 51% of its bilateral budget funds to Africa (BMZ, 2015a). Among Germany's 50 partner countries, 22 are in Africa and 25 are least developed countries or other low-income countries.

Despite the stated focus on Africa, 32% of Germany's total bilateral allocable ODA went to countries in Africa in 2013, while 34% went to countries in Asia (Table B.3). This results from the fact that allocation criteria only concern BMZ budget funds, while Germany's total ODA allocations include KfW's overall concessional lending activity. As a development bank using market resources, KfW offers financial products to meet the needs of countries at various income levels. Therefore, KfW uses its own resources to finance a range of loans at different concessionality levels, which translates into a significant volume of concessional loans going to more developed, mostly Asian, middle-income countries (Box 3.1).

At the same time, Germany restricts financial co-operation with least developed countries to grants. As a result, in 2013, only 27% of bilateral country-allocable ODA went to least developed countries and other low-income countries, while 73% went to middle-income countries (Figure 3.3 and Table B.3). The amount of bilateral ODA allocated to least developed and low-income countries is actually lower than it was in 2012 (40%) and 2009 (30%).

Box 3.1 KfW Development Bank: sources of funds and financing instruments

In addition to budget funds from BMZ, KfW uses its own resources to deploy a range of financing instruments customised to partner countries' financial capabilities and the specific economic characteristics of individual projects. BMZ finances approximately one-third of KfW's ODA-eligible operations in the form of grants to least developed countries, loans at terms of the International Development Association (IDA), and part of development loans with interest subsidies.

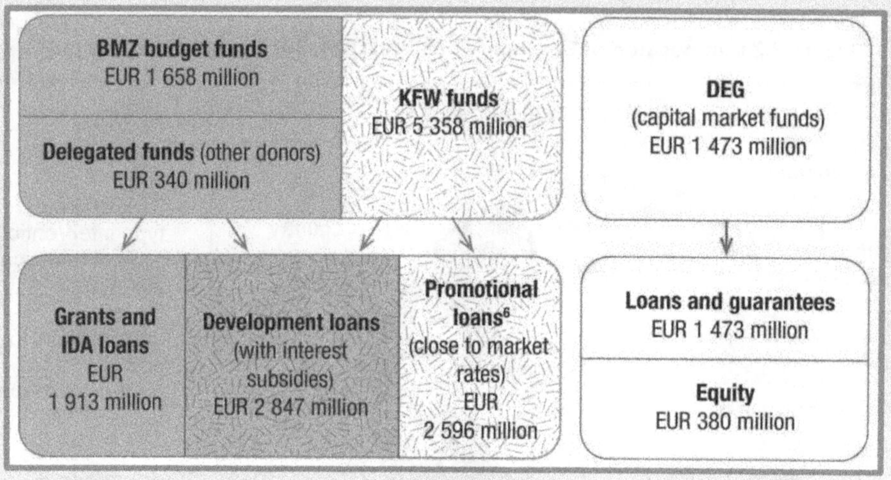

Source: Handouts prepared by KfW for the DAC peer review

Figure 3.3 Germany's share of bilateral allocable ODA by income group, 2009-13

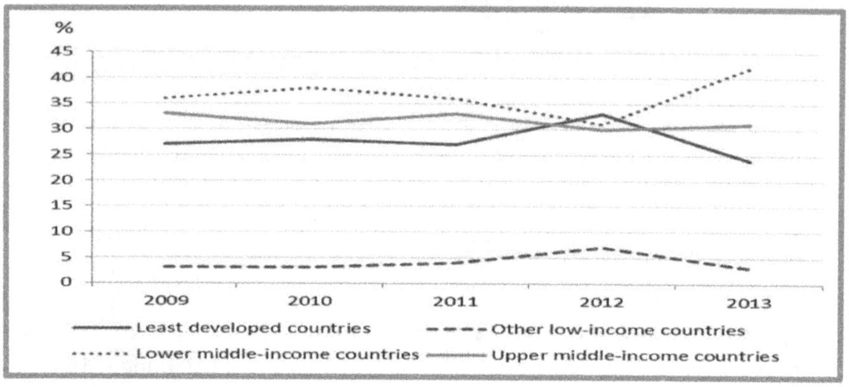

Source: DAC statistics.

Sector allocations emphasise poverty reduction, governance, economic growth and the environment

Sector allocations reflect Germany's focus on poverty reduction, good governance and a socially and ecologically oriented market economy. The largest share of German gross bilateral ODA commitments goes to social infrastructure and services (43% in 2012-13), with a particular focus on education, government and civil society. This is followed by economic infrastructure and services (27% in 2012-13), with a strong focus on energy, banking and financial services (Table B.5).

Germany's emphasis on the environment is also visible in its sector allocations, with multisector aid (13% in 2012-13 average) reflecting its action in climate investment (mitigation and adaptation), biodiversity and sustainable management of natural resources. Germany is also investing in the environment and climate in other areas such as energy, agriculture and water. Indeed, the share of German bilateral aid focusing on the environment reached 40% in 2013, well above the DAC country average of 23%.

Germany's commitment to climate change mitigation and adaptation has also increased considerably in 2010 and 2011 before stabilising in 2012 and 2013 at 28% of its bilateral ODA, compared to a DAC country average of 17% (OECD, 2015a).

Multilateral ODA channel

Indicator: The member uses the multilateral aid channel effectively

Germany engages constructively with multilateral organisations. It gives priority to core contributions in accordance with its strategy to help these organisations deliver their mandate effectively. In recent years, Germany has increased its earmarked contributions, while its overall ODA channelled to multilateral organisations has decreased.

The share of ODA to multilateral organisations has fallen

In 2013, Germany allocated 29% of its total gross ODA as core contributions to multilateral organisations, slightly higher than the DAC country average of 27%. Since 2009, however, Germany's share of multilateral ODA in total gross ODA has decreased from 37% (Table B.2). In addition, Germany allocated a further 7% of its bilateral ODA for specific projects implemented by multilateral organisations (multi-bi/non-core contributions).

As the biggest economy in the EU, Germany is the most important contributor to the European Union budget and to the European Development Fund (EDF). Germany provides some USD 2.5 billion each year to the development co-operation budget managed by the EU. Germany is also an important contributor to the World Bank group and to UN agencies. Contributions to other multilateral agencies – mainly the Global Fund to Fight AIDS, Tuberculosis and Malaria – are relatively large (Figure 3.4).

Germany prioritises core contributions to multilateral organisations

Germany is giving priority to core contributions to multilateral organisations in accordance with its strategy to help these organisations deliver their mandate effectively. It remains among the DAC members providing the smallest share of its gross ODA in earmarked funding to multilateral organisations (OECD, 2015b). However, Germany's share of bilateral aid channelled through multilateral organisations as earmarked or non-core contributions has increased in recent years (Figure 3.4). This increase consists mainly of non-core funding to UN Funds and Programmes, which doubled in 2013 due to Germany's humanitarian response to the Syrian crisis.

Figure 3.4 Germany's core and non-core allocations to multilateral organisations, 2011-13

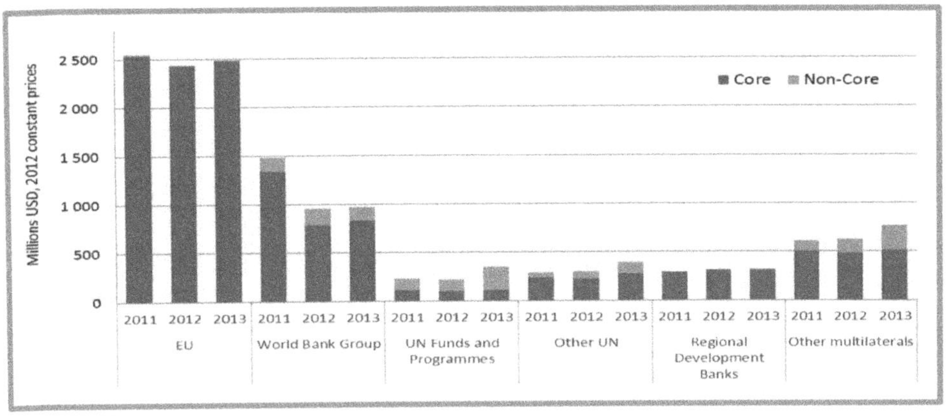

Source: DAC statistics

Notes

1. Source: OECD Compare your country website (www.compareyourcountry.org/oda), accessed 15 May 2015.
2. The government made this announcement on the occasion of adopting a revised budget for 2015, together with a financial plan up to 2019 (BMZ, 2015b).
3. With a budget increase of EUR 860 million in 2016, this also represents the largest increase ever for BMZ.
4. Although Germany has reaffirmed its commitment to the 0.7% target, the lack of a timeframe for achieving it represents a setback in light of the EU commitment of 0.51% by 2010 and 0.7% by 2015.
5. For information on the 1978 Recommendation on the Terms and Conditions of Aid, see: www.oecd.org/dac/stats/31426776.pdf .
6. Partner countries benefit from a full programme of bilateral co-operation, with up to three priority sectors per country. Germany also engages in co-operation activities in a further 29 countries under a thematic or regional programme and only one priority area per country (BMZ, 2015a).
7. Country programmable aid is the proportion of ODA over which partner countries have, or could have, significant say. For information see: www.oecd.org/dac/aid-architecture/countryprogrammableaidcpafrequentlyaskedquestions.htm.

Bibliography

Government sources

BMZ (2015a), *OECD DAC Peer Review of Germany 2015 – Memorandum by Germany*, BMZ, Bonn.

BMZ (2015b), *Höchste Steigerung und höchster Etat in der Geschichte des Entwicklungsministeriums* (highest budget increase and highest budget in the history of BMZ), Press Release, 18 March 2015, (in German), available at: www.bmz.de/20150318-2, BMZ, Bonn.

Other sources

Busan Partnership for Effective Development Co-operation (2011), endorsed at the Fourth High-Level Forum on Aid Effectiveness, Busan, Republic of Korea, 29 November-1 December 2011, available at: http://effectivecooperation.org.

OECD (2015a), Development Co-operation Report 2015, OECD, Paris.

OECD (2015b), *Multilateral Aid 2015: Better Partnerships for a Post-2015 World*, OECD, Paris.

OECD (2014a), *2014 Global Outlook on Aid: Results of the 2014 DAC Survey on Donors' Forward Spending Plans and Prospects for Improving Aid Predictability*, OECD, Paris, available at: www.oecd.org/dac/aid-architecture/GlobalOutlookAid-web.pdf.

OECD (2014b), *DAC HLM Final Communiqué*, 16 December 2014, OECD, Paris, available at: www.oecd.org/dac/OECD%20DAC%20HLM%20Communique.pdf.

Chapter 4: Managing Germany's development co-operation

Institutional system

Indicator: The institutional structure is conducive to consistent, quality development co-operation

Germany has taken further steps to streamline its institutional system. It has done so for policy by strengthening the Ministry for Economic Co-operation and Development (BMZ), and for implementation by merging three technical co-operation agencies to create GIZ. Germany now needs to revisit formal processes and refine BMZ's business model to reinforce its steering function on German development co-operation and ensure that systems and procedures support context-based, flexible approaches in the field.

There are on-going efforts to streamline the development co-operation system

While Germany has taken steps to further streamline its complex development co-operation system, key features have remained unchanged for a decade (Figure 4.1):

- a dedicated ministry (BMZ), represented at cabinet level, leads on development co-operation policy;
- A wide range of German stakeholders implement Germany's development policy. These include two powerful agencies (GIZ and KfW),[1] as well as other government ministries, federal states, political foundations, church-based organisations, NGOs, scientific and training institutions;[2]
- Financial and technical co-operation have separate budgets and are implemented by different institutions;
- In partner countries, BMZ is represented through staff seconded to embassies and other key stakeholders (e.g. GIZ, KfW) have their own representations.

Figure 4.1 The German institutional system for development co-operation

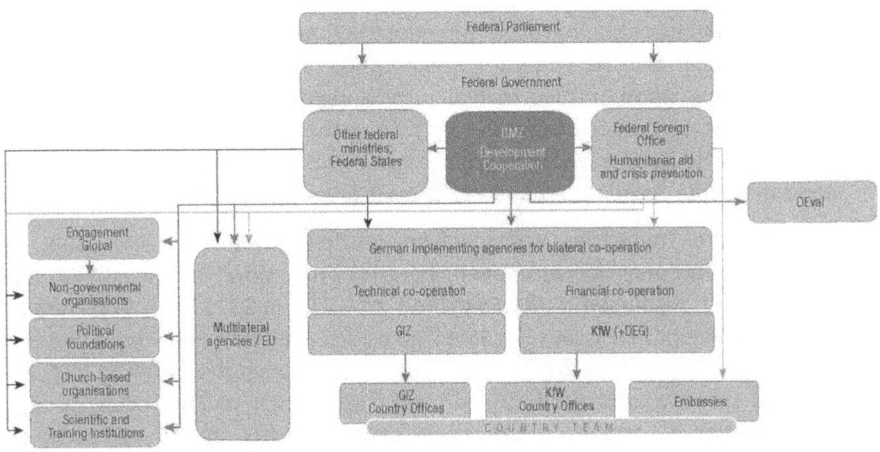

Source: based on information provided to the review team

In line with the recommendations of the 2010 peer review, Germany has taken steps to streamline its system and making it fit for addressing future challenges. This has involved strengthening BMZ, consolidating humanitarian assistance within the Federal Foreign Office (Chapter 7), merging three technical agencies, and making efforts to manage arrangements between development co-operation policy and delivery functions efficiently.

BMZ now has a clear mandate to set policy and oversee German development co-operation,[3] and it has enhanced its capacity to fulfil its mandate. BMZ's strengthening has involved reinforcing its political leadership with the nomination of a second Parliamentary State Secretary to engage further with Parliament and the public. In addition, BMZ was reorganised in 2014 to increase its efficiency as well as to ensure the implementation of the new main political focal points: the 2030 Agenda; climate change, and the special initiative, "One world – no hunger". This was done by creating dedicated units for each of these areas.[4] Finally, over the last five years, BMZ has strengthened its policy capacity, increasing its staff numbers at headquarters by 27% (with 165 new positions). At the same time, 46 additional staff members were seconded to embassies to oversee the development co-operation programme – a 78% increase.

In 2011, three agencies, GTZ (technical co-operation), InWEnt (human resource development and training) and DED (volunteer services and secondments) were merged into a new organisation, GIZ. The merger is bearing fruit. As the review team noted in Mozambique and Kenya, it has led to increased efficiencies and greater strategic coherence, while retaining the comparative advantages of each instrument and sharpening their use. Meanwhile some 15% of GIZ's activities are now commissioned by ministries other than BMZ. The fact that ministries involved in development co-operation work with GIZ and KfW can help ensure coherence in Germany's overall approach to development.

BMZ's clear mandate and enhanced capacity result in a better balance between the policy and implementation functions of German development co-operation. There is greater clarity over BMZ's role in relation to the two major implementing agencies, GIZ, who manages technical co-operation, and KfW, responsible for financial co-operation. BMZ now has a clear policy steering role at headquarters; meanwhile in the field, its increased staffing seconded to embassies also means that heads of co-operation can lead on policy dialogue with partner governments and other development stakeholders. Increasing staff in embassies also helps to inform decision making by BMZ (Annex C).

Opportunities exist for enhancing cross-government work on development

Co-ordination has also improved between BMZ, responsible for nearly half of German ODA (47% in 2013), and the Federal Foreign Office (in charge of 12% of ODA in 2013),[5] with clearer demarcation of roles, including for humanitarian assistance. This is having positive results, illustrated by the German response to the 2014 Ebola crisis. However, more can be done to maximise the synergies among these two ministries' instruments and ensure more consistent approaches in areas such as crisis prevention and recovery (Chapter 7).

Several other ministries are involved in development co-operation, although they individually account for a smaller share of ODA flows. For example, the Ministry of Environment disbursed EUR 165 million of ODA in 2013[6]. Cross-government work on specific development issues is guided by a series of inter-ministerial strategic guidelines,[7] as well as co-operation agreements[8] and co-ordination mechanisms (e.g. a working party on food security co-chaired by BMZ and the Ministry of Food Security and Agriculture). Co-ordination is particularly intense on peace and security[9] as well as on climate change issues, two aspects that require even further inter-ministerial collaboration (Chapter 1). Co-ordination takes place at both policy and technical levels, and can be theme-based (e.g. food security) or country focused (e.g. Afghanistan).

The key positions of the German government for the post-2015 agenda set in August 2013 and December 2014 (Federal Government, 2014) and the Charter for the Future (BMZ, 2014) have the potential to enhance cross-government work on development. BMZ should build on these important statements and take advantage of its recent strengthening to improve the consistency of all development co-operation activities. This requires overseeing ODA-related activities implemented by other ministries as well as federal states and local governments more systematically, consistent with BMZ's mandate to co-ordinate overall ODA funding. So far BMZ has taken a pragmatic approach to co-ordination, setting up ad hoc committees as needed. Looking ahead, it should consider whether other organisational arrangements could support whole-of-government approaches better in the German context.

Clear division of labour facilitates operational co-ordination in partner countries

In partner countries, Germany is taking steps to adopt comprehensive joined-up approaches involving different actors and tools in a number of areas. In Kenya, where Germany has a broad portfolio (which includes Somalia), the embassy has several co-ordination mechanisms which bring together all German stakeholders, including the political foundations (Annex C). There are effective synergies in areas such as private sector development and peace and conflict. As in other partner countries, all German ministries engaged in development co-operation are involved in government-to-government consultation and negotiation.

Operational co-ordination is aided by the clearer division of labour between BMZ and the implementing agencies, the establishment of country teams[10] and – in most partner countries – the fact that GIZ and KfW offices are located in a common "German House". Staff from BMZ seconded in embassies lead on policy dialogue, drawing on the expertise of the implementing agencies. In Kenya and Mozambique, the different German institutions, instruments and tools work in a coherent way, seeking synergies with programmes designed jointly at the sector level. Flexibility and good information sharing are essential for this to work effectively. While the latter relies on individuals to a great extent, guidance from headquarters is useful to generate shared understanding and facilitate complementary interventions. This is the case on capacity development, where GIZ and KfW share a joint approach (Chapter 5).

In fragile environments, while Germany does have flexibility to design programmes that are context-specific and context-sensitive, the institutional divide between technical and financial co-operation could limit its ability to adjust programmes as quickly as required in these rapidly evolving environments.

BMZ's business model now needs to be revised to speed up systems and increase in-country autonomy

Taking advantage of the recent institutional reforms, Germany should now revisit formal processes in order to introduce flexibility to adjust programming and procedures based on conditions on the ground, without compromising quality and integrity.

Following its reorganisation in 2014, BMZ has engaged in a task assessment. This review could be a step in revisiting BMZ's business model to:

- Ensure that policy priorities are strongly integrated within the ministry's work, are adequately resourced and are complementary. For instance, it is not clear how the three newly-created units (on the 2030 Agenda; climate change, and the special initiative, "One world – no hunger") link to the work of the five BMZ directorates.

- Streamline systems and procedures in headquarters: processes are time consuming and the resulting delays undermine implementation in the field (e.g. half of the country strategies have not yet been issued). Bottlenecks need to be identified and addressed. For example, reducing the numerous clearance layers could help rationalise work. This would allow staff to be reallocated to where they are most needed.
- Delegate more authority to the field: this was recommended by the 2010 DAC peer review (OECD, 2011) and would be a logical next step in the reform process now that more BMZ staff have been seconded to embassies. As seen in Mozambique and Kenya, centralised decision making lengthens the programming process and risks resulting in lack of flexibility, undermining the quality of partnerships. Decentralising decision-making responsibilities, accompanied by adequate resources, would improve BMZ's strategic oversight of Germany's ODA and could help to address some partners' concerns about delays in processing decisions and approvals.

BMZ has launched a two-year pilot in eight partner countries, delegating greater responsibility to staff seconded to embassies for developing country strategies and preparing government negotiations. The results of this pilot will be assessed jointly by BMZ and the Federal Foreign Office, paving the way for the latter ministry's close involvement in the next steps. This was the approach taken in 2012 when the two ministries designed the modalities for increasing BMZ staff seconded to embassies.[11] Indeed, delegating further authority for policy and strategy to staff in the field will require revising the understanding on working relationships between BMZ and the Federal Foreign Office.

According to the 2012 agreement between BMZ and the Federal Foreign Office, BMZ staff seconded to embassies become part of the foreign service, and report officially to the Federal Foreign Office. Therefore, while BMZ and other ministries may receive copies of the exchanges of information between the Federal Foreign Office and the embassies, there is no direct formal communication between BMZ headquarters and the staff working on development co-operation in the embassies. While this system may foster consistency in Germany's approach to partner countries, it creates challenges by complicating the information and feedback loop between BMZ and the implementing agencies at headquarters and in the field. As they design the contours of the new decentralised model, BMZ and the Federal Foreign Office should consider ways to reduce transaction costs and accelerate consultation, control and decision-making processes.

As regards implementing agencies, GIZ is largely decentralised. Meanwhile KfW's business model and its limited number of staff posted in country offices mean that project management of financial co-operation largely occurs at headquarters. KfW has started to increase its staffing in partner countries, and should consider the pros and cons of delegating further authority to country offices, backed up by additional resources and greater empowerment for local managers. This is relevant to adjust the agency to future needs, considering that the demand for decentralisation is likely to grow as more countries develop their capacity to engage with development partners.

Adaptation to change

Indicator: The system is able to reform and innovate to meet evolving needs

The major stakeholders in Germany's development co-operation have adapted to the significant reforms of the last five years, proving their ability to manage change effectively. Germany also encourages creativity and this translates into a number of innovative approaches for making the most of opportunities as they arise.

Constant change monitoring has smoothed the reform process

The reforms carried out by Germany's three major development co-operation stakeholders – BMZ, GIZ and KfW – over the last five years have shown that these organisations can manage change effectively.

The new structure arising from BMZ's series of reforms over recent years seems clear to BMZ staff, who feel that they were well informed and appropriately involved in these processes. However, feedback from staff also reveals that individual workload is perceived as high, mostly at lower levels. New processes take time to be fully implemented (e.g. BMZ introduced a new format for country strategies in 2012, yet only half of them were finalised by the end of 2014). This calls for streamlining systems and procedures.

GIZ's creation from the merger of three technical agencies is nearly finished. The various instruments of the former agencies have now been fully integrated within headquarters and sector management lines in most partner countries (e.g. Kenya). GIZ is aware, however, of the cultural gap between the three previous entities. This still needs to be looked at as it consolidates its organisation. GIZ also needs to find a way to manage "development workers" more flexibly. These German volunteers have now been integrated into GIZ programmes in partner countries, meaning they can no longer be moved from one country to another as they used to be when managed under a specific DED budget line. Having a regional fund may allow for a more flexible use of volunteers, which could be useful in volatile contexts.

KfW was reorganised in 2013 to adapt to the new instruments and deliver the programme more effectively and efficiently. A Change Management Office was created to support the reform through appropriate communication to staff, guidance for managers and mechanisms to monitor progress. For instance, a "modernisation barometer" was introduced in the form of a regular short staff survey online to keep track of the effects of change management measures. This re-organisation is now complete. Thanks to leaner procedures, upgraded information technology, redeployment of expertise and the set-up of tendering units, KfW was able to manage a significant scale-up in ODA volume without increasing staffing levels.

Creativity and innovation are valued

Germany seeks innovation in both policy and implementation as a way of responding appropriately to changes in the development landscape. BMZ is at the forefront in developing new co-operation models to engage with emerging economies, including triangular co-operation (Chapter 5). GIZ and KfW's management also value creativity and strive to strengthen staff capacity for innovation. As an illustration, every two years GIZ holds an agency-wide gender competition to stimulate innovations in this field. This approach to innovation has enabled GIZ and KfW to support promising ideas worldwide, such as mobile banking for rural populations in African countries; results-based financing pilots in sectors as diverse as energy, health and water as well as new models of public-private partnerships. Innovation applies also to learning and tracking impact, illustrated by a tool developed by KfW to assess the employment effects of its entire portfolio (KfW, 2015).

Human resources

Indicator: The member manages its human resources effectively to respond to field imperatives

The German institutions are making efforts to match their staff to needs. BMZ has been managing a substantial increase in staff, while the implementing agencies have been improving the professional development of their staff. To ensure staff seconded to embassies have the right skills, BMZ should offer appropriate incentives and increase opportunities for learning. Meanwhile KfW could consider making better use of the capacities of its locally recruited staff. This could help to delegate more authority to the field in an efficient way.

Germany is taking steps to encourage the right staff levels and skills in the right places

BMZ has substantially increased its staffing numbers to fulfil its extended mandate and compensate for the support previously provided by GIZ.[12] Its staff numbers at headquarters increased by 27% between 2009 and 2014 and staff seconded to embassies increased by 78% (46 posts) (Figure 4.2). BMZ's task assessment should now help the ministry to ensure it has the right staff in the right places – both at headquarters and in the field, including in fragile contexts. This was clearly not the case for Somalia, where 50% of one BMZ seconded staff based in Nairobi embassy was allocated to cover the entire Somalia portfolio,[13] resulting in a high workload and limiting Germany's involvement in donor co-ordination mechanisms in Somalia (Annex C). Such examples emphasise the need to match staff presence in partner countries (or in neighbouring countries, as in the case of Somalia/Kenya) to the size and complexity of portfolios.

As heads of co-operation in partner countries, staff from BMZ seconded to embassies have extended responsibilities for managing the policy dialogue with partner countries and other development partners, setting policy orientations and overseeing the various German actors engaged in delivering the programme. As part of the task assessment, BMZ should ensure the incentives are appropriate to secure people with the right skills and level of experience for these jobs, especially in difficult environments. This includes reconsidering the positioning of these posts within the grading structure and career path.

In 2014, GIZ employed a total of 15 251 staff on its public sector business (excluding activities managed by GIZ International Services)[14] (Figure 4.2). This number has remained quite stable over the last five years, considering the merger (in 2009 there was a total of 15 504 staff across GTZ, DED and InWEnt). A large share of GIZ international staff (40%) is posted in its 90 country offices. In addition, GIZ employs more than 10 000 locally recruited staff – they represent more than two-thirds of total GIZ staff. GIZ pursues a single workforce policy, in which the skills of international seconded staff and locally-recruited staff complement each other and all staff benefit from the same personnel policy principles.[15] GIZ's national staff policy aims to strengthen human resources management of locally-recruited staff in country offices, developing their competences and their employability on the market. GIZ provides a fulfilling career path for locally-recruited staff: 12% of such staff are in managerial or senior professional posts, and another 41% have specialist and managerial duties (GIZ, 2014).

Like GIZ, KfW's staff numbers have remained stable over the last five years although numbers are much lower, reflecting the specificity of financial co-operation compared to technical co-operation. KfW's centralised model is reflected in the limited number of staff posted in partner countries. It has 79 staff members posted across nearly 70 country offices, along with 290 locally-recruited staff with limited management responsibilities. While KfW has developed a solid approach to human resource management, career development opportunities for local staff are constrained. KfW could consider ways to further integrate and empower local staff so as to make full use of their capacities and support decentralisation.[16]

Figure 4.2 Staff numbers in BMZ, GIZ and KfW, 2014

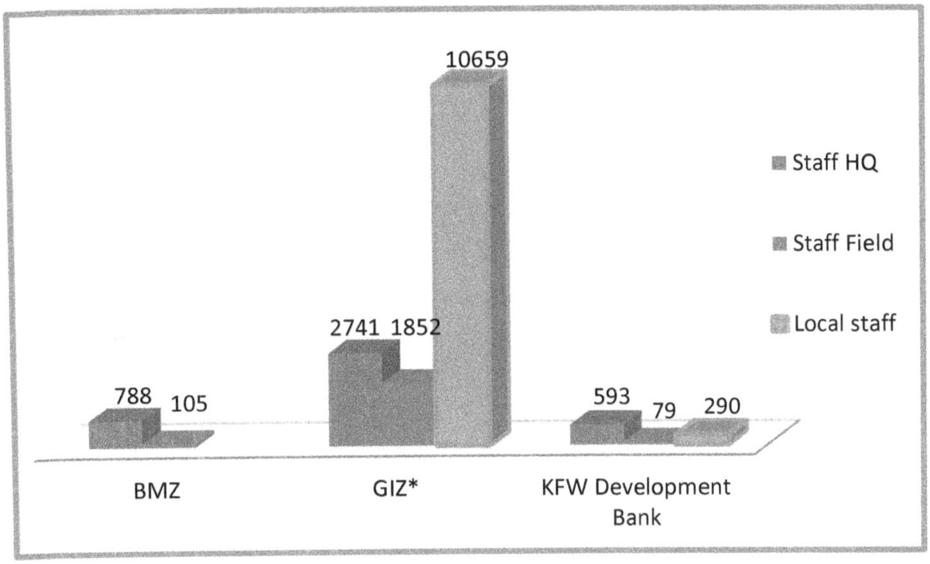

Note:*Figures exclude staff working in GIZ International Services. GIZ national personnel are reported as head count numbers; other figures are full-time equivalent.

Source: data shared with the review team.

Germany invests in staff skills through appropriate incentives and training

BMZ renewed personal development policy aims to absorb its new staff and develop their skills. As part of this policy, managers assess staff skills every two years, a process used to consider opportunities for promoting or moving staff to other positions. The new policy has also involved a threefold increase in the training budget. Training is now an integral part of the annual talks between staff and managers. Holding managers accountable for the development of their staff could be made more systematic, however, by reflecting this in their own performance assessments. BMZ should also consider how to accompany its strengthened presence in embassies with a commensurate access to learning and exchange opportunities, in order to reinforce staff capacities in piloting development co-operation in the field. In addition, it could be useful to create ways to exchange lessons between staff located in different fragile environments.

Recognising the crucial role of their staff, GIZ and KfW have created a positive working and learning culture, supported by a wide range of training – including on-line training – and systems to identify talents and promote staff. GIZ has a talent management scheme to harness its staff's potential and strengthen capacities. Similarly, KfW introduced a new management system for senior managers in 2009 to identify and monitor talented employees systematically. The review team noted the positive impact of this culture in Kenya and Mozambique, where the expertise and commitment of German staff are widely appreciated (Annex C).

Notes

1. GIZ is an entirely government-owned federal enterprise, supporting the German Government in achieving its sustainable development objectives. In 2013, GIZ's budget was over EUR 1.9 billion, with commissions from BMZ amounting to EUR 1.4 billion. The second largest commissioning ministry after BMZ was the German Federal Foreign Office, with EUR 119 million, followed by the Ministry of Environment with EUR 87 million. GIZ operates in about 130 countries worldwide, in about 90 offices (GIZ, 2014). As an integral part of the KfW group, KfW Development Bank carries out Germany's financial co-operation with developing countries on behalf of the federal government. In 2014, it managed EUR 1.66 billion from the federal budget. In addition, it raised EUR 5.36 billion on the capital market to finance development programmes in developing countries (KfW, 2014).

2. Federal states and local governments channel most of their support (USD 1.02 billion in 2013) through training institutions and research institutes (USD 856 million in 2013). The majority of this support consists of imputed student costs (Table C.2).

3. The preface of the BMZ "Departmental budget 23" of the 2014 Federal budget clearly states that, within "the German government, the BMZ co-ordinates Germany's official development assistance (ODA). The BMZ is responsible for the bulk of German ODA funding."

4. See the organisational chart in Annex 3 of the Memorandum of Germany (BMZ, 2015).

5. BMZ disbursed USD 5.13 billion and the Federal Foreign Office USD 1.28 billion out of a total of USD 10.85 billion of German ODA in 2013 (2012 prices).

6. Other ministries involved are the Ministry of Food security and agriculture and the Ministry of Education and research.

7. For instance the *Federal Government Policy Guidelines for Africa* (FFO, 2014), the *Federal Government guidelines on shaping globalisation* (FFO, 2012), and the *inter-ministerial guidelines on fragile states* agreed by the Federal Foreign Office, the Ministry of Defence and BMZ (FFO/MD/BMZ, 2012).

8. For instance, a co-operation agreement between the Ministry of Food Security and BMZ ensures a co-ordinated approach to food security when dealing with international organisations and in partner countries.

9. The secretaries of state from the Chancellery, Ministry of Defence, Federal Foreign Office and BMZ meet every three months to co-ordinate their positions in conflict situations such as Iraq, Mali and the Central African Republic.

10. Country teams are made up of the embassy development co-operation team (Head of Co-operation and Deputy Head of Co-operation), plus GIZ and KfW Country Directors, and Focal Co-ordinators.

11. Consultations between BMZ and the Federal Foreign Office led to an agreement on the secondment of staff from BMZ to the Federal Foreign Office, signed in September 2012. This defines the respective responsibilities of the two ministries, and contains human resources, financing and procedural provisions to guide staff secondment.

12. Before 2010 staff from GIZ were posted within BMZ to help the ministry deliver on its ministerial tasks. This practice stopped following a request by the Court of Auditors.

13. In 2014, EUR 90 million were ready to be used for German-Somali development co-operation.

14. GIZ International Services – or GIZ IS – is an independent operational department of GIZ that provides services to clients such as international institutions, governments from developed countries and private businesses.

15. GIZ recognises that, as well as having professional sector knowledge, national staff understand the political and socio-cultural contexts and have access to a broad range of social contacts that can be key to success.

16. As for other German stakeholders, the requirement for key documents to be in German inevitably imposes some limitations on opportunities for local staff advancement.

Bibliography

Government sources

BMZ (2015), *OECD DAC Peer Review of Germany 2015 – Memorandum by Germany, BMZ, Bonn.*

BMZ (2014), *Charter for the Future - One world, Our Responsibility,* BMZ, Bonn.

Federal Government (2014), *Post-2015 Agenda for Sustainable Development - Key positions of the German government*, Federal Government Berlin, available at: https://sustainabledevelopment.un.org/content/documents/8778germany.pdf.

FFO (2014), *Federal Government Policy Guidelines for Africa*, Federal Foreign Office, Berlin, www.auswaertiges-amt.de/cae/servlet/contentblob/677752/publicationFile/195378/140521_Afrika-Leitlinien-Download.pdf.

FFO (2012), *Shaping Globalization – Expanding Partnerships – Sharing Responsibility, A Strategy Paper by the German Government*, Federal Foreign Office, Berlin, available at: www.auswaertiges-amt.de/cae/servlet/contentblob/616584/publicationFile/190244/Gestaltungsmaechtekonzept%20engl.pdf.

FFO/MD/BMZ (2012), *For a Coherent German Policy Towards Fragile States – Inter-ministerial guidelines*, September 2014, Berlin.

GIZ (2014), *Company Report 2013. GIZ. Solutions that work, Deutsche Gesellschaft für Internationale Zusammenarbeit,* Bonn, available at https://www.giz.de/en/downloads/giz2014-en-annual-report-2013.pdf.

KfW (2015), "Employment effects of financial co-operation: an estimation model", KfW Position Paper, January 2015, Frankfurt, available at: www.kfw-entwicklungsbank.de/PDF/Download-Center/PDF-Dokumente-Positionspapiere/2015_01_22_PP_-Besch%C3%A4ftigungsmodell_EN.pdf.

KfW (2014), *Annual Report 2013*, KfW, Frankfurt.

Other sources

OECD (2011), *OECD Development Assistance Peer Reviews: Germany 2010*, OECD Publishing, Paris, available at: http://dx.doi.org/10.1787/9789264098299-en.

Chapter 5: Germany's development co-operation delivery and partnerships

Budgeting and programming processes

Indicator: These processes support quality aid as defined in Busan

BMZ is increasing the predictability of German aid through multi-year commitments, but it could share long-term spending information more systematically with partner countries and has yet to finalise country strategies for more than half its partner countries since introducing a new template in 2012. While BMZ is increasingly combining technical and financial co-operation in an effective way, greater budget flexibility would help German development co-operation to adapt to evolving needs. Use of country systems varies across sectors and modalities, preventing Germany from meeting its commitment to make use of country systems the default approach. While technical co-operation is appreciated by partners, there may be benefits in using the various German instruments more flexibly and maximising the role of partner structures in programme implementation.

Multi-year predictability is improving but budget flexibility remains limited

Germany's annual budgeting process provides the framework for BMZ to determine commitments and spending during the year. The ministry can make binding multi-annual payment commitments to partner countries, including for contributions to budget support and other programme-based approaches, which, however, require prior individual approval from Parliament. BMZ prepares indicative spending plans based on existing commitments with a three-year horizon, reporting to DAC forward spending surveys (Chapter 3). While Germany shares information on planned disbursements for the next programming cycle during bilateral negotiations with partner country governments, it only provides additional information for future years when partners request such information (OECD, 2014a). Although country strategies bring further predictability, Germany could do more to share information systematically with partner countries, however, and make it available three to five years ahead on a rolling basis.[1]

The fixed resource allocations for financial and technical co-operation, each with their own dedicated budget lines, make the system rigid and may have implications for programming choices. Individual programmes would also benefit from greater flexibility in reallocating funds across budget lines and years so as to adapt to evolving situations. The introduction of the special initiatives in 2014 (Chapter 2) is a major change in BMZ's way of working. While these initiatives introduce thematic and sector priorities without pre-determining the channels for resource allocation - namely whether it will involve bilateral or multilateral co-operation, technical or financial co-operation, as well as NGOs - feedback from various stakeholders suggests that their initial experience in applying for funding from these initiatives has proven challenging, especially the requirement to disburse funds according to a fixed timeline (Annex C). In consolidating the procedures for managing these initiatives, BMZ will need to review carefully how to make the most of the flexibility inherent in these initiatives without compromising the coherence of existing country programmes with separate planning and reporting requirements.

Programming processes support alignment with national strategies but speeding up the preparation of country strategies would benefit strategic planning

In 2012, in response to a recommendation in the 2010 peer review, BMZ changed its approach to country strategies in order to strengthen internal planning, and especially to enhance its results focus (Annex A). These strategies, which cover a period of up to seven years, are the main multi-annual planning document for setting strategic priorities and allocating resources.[2] They also increase predictability when they include indicative medium-term budget figures - however, indicative spending plans are mandatory only for countries where EU joint programming initiatives are under way. BMZ should speed up the finalisation of country strategies for all its partner countries – currently available for less than half of Germany's partner countries - given the importance of these documents for longer-term planning and predictability.

Bilateral negotiations, which BMZ organises every two or three years with partner country governments, are the basis for shaping German development co-operation programmes. Agreements arising from these bilateral negotiations enable BMZ to mandate GIZ and KfW to develop concrete project proposals for financial and technical co-operation through a commissioning procedure. Germany's support is aligned to priorities of partner countries. In Kenya and Mozambique, the selection of focus sectors within Germany's broader priorities has remained stable over time, a feature making Germany a reliable partner and able to draw on experience to achieve better impact (Annex C). At the same time, the review team found that BMZ could benefit from periodic portfolio reviews to assess the overall relevance and effectiveness of its approaches in a country and inform its future programming choices, instead of allowing current programmes to unduly influence decision making (Chapter 6).

In accordance with the recommendation of the 2010 peer review, Germany is moving towards a more comprehensive approach to capacity development, combining action of both technical and financial co-operation (Annex A). GIZ is also ensuring that technical co-operation responds better to partner country demand (Box 5.1). Despite its stronger focus on results (Chapter 6), GIZ may need to reflect further on how to ensure that its approach builds explicit time-bound performance milestones into programmes and defines phasing out measures. In this context, BMZ would also need to look at technical co-operation from a "value for money" perspective, identifying different ways of achieving similar results, including through accessing different forms and sources of advice and expertise as well as strengthening partner countries' own systems by using them.

Germany needs to look more systematically for opportunities to use country systems as the default approach

The 2010 peer review recommended that Germany make greater use of partner country systems and adapt its aid instruments to programme-based approaches (Annex A). BMZ shows strong commitment to using partner countries' systems and plays an active role in shaping international dialogue within the Effective Institutions Platform. However, less than half of Germany's aid flows are reported as being on partner countries' budgets or as using their national budget procedures (OECD/UNDP, 2014). Germany provides general budget support to four partner countries, down from twelve countries in 2010, due to political reasons; it also makes limited contributions to pooled programmes and funds. It needs to make more effort to increase the use of country systems wherever possible in line with the Busan commitments (2011) of using country systems as the default option. Within financial co-operation, country systems are used extensively. However, it is important that when KfW puts in place additional safeguards, as it does in Kenya – justifiably – it reviews the need for having them over time. Similarly, when strengthening country systems through specific capacity development programmes, GIZ needs to consider how to use its various technical co-operation instruments to maximise the role of partner countries' structures and systems in programme implementation. In this context, Germany is well placed to share experience and stimulate further thinking on how best to adjust technical co-operation with a view to building institutional capacities to support the implementation of the SDGs.

Box 5.1 Germany's approach to capacity development

Germany is increasingly designing joint technical and financial co-operation programmes, an approach which has proven instrumental for developing synergies and piloting approaches that can be replicated – for example in the education sector in Mozambique. Germany adopts a multi-level approach to capacity development: advising ministries on implementing sector plans or supporting their reforms (macro level); advising local authorities in delivering services (intermediate level); and piloting projects (micro level).

With its greater focus on results, BMZ's commissioning process with GIZ and KfW allows for greater flexibility, with emphasis on outputs rather than inputs, thus making it easier for GIZ and KfW to adjust project implementation to the actual needs of partner countries. The merger of different technical co-operation agencies is also helping GIZ to use its various instruments more flexibly to match the needs of its partners (Chapter 4). While GIZ and KfW do their best to jointly develop mutually supportive programmes, the fixed resource allocation between financial and technical co-operation may prevent Germany from adjusting its mix of instruments to fully respond to country priorities and contexts when making programming choices. In addition, the different project durations of the two instruments (three years for technical co-operation and up to seven years for financial co-operation), reduces synergies and undermines the longer-term perspective needed to build national capacities and ensure sustainability.

GIZ ensures that partners play an active role in implementing programmes by steering projects jointly with partner governments and locating programme offices in government premises. However, the fact that GIZ is an implementing agency with fully-fledged teams directly responsible for implementing projects, inevitably creates parallel systems and limits the extent to which programmes can use government structures and processes.

As BMZ reviews its guidance on country systems,[3] it should consider how to make greater use of these systems beyond public financial management and procurement, especially for modalities other than budget support. It can build on its experience of engaging in sector-wide approaches through a mix of complementary instruments and modalities. Germany could lead by example in demonstrating how to align project-based assistance better with country systems by integrating projects into programme-based approaches (Box 5.2). Where country systems cannot be used as the default approach, Germany should consider options for strengthening those systems, taking advantage of its technical co-operation tools. Where there are serious concerns about fiduciary risks, as in Kenya (Annex C), Germany should take advantage of its lead role on anti-corruption as well as donor co-ordination structures to discuss and identify jointly with the government priority issues for strengthening country systems. Such dialogue would be critical to help build trust so that donors can gradually increase their use of country systems.

Germany has a sound approach to risk management, including corruption

Germany systematically analyses different types of risks and uses the analysis, including mitigation measures, to design and manage its programmes. BMZ has increased its emphasis on risk in fragile states. In countries where deteriorating security affects programme implementation, BMZ and the Federal Foreign Office have set up a Risk Management Office to support staff. In Kenya the review team noted that Germany was doing a good job of integrating conflict sensitivity and factors exacerbating fragility – such as corruption – into its country analysis and monitoring processes. Germany is undergoing a major reform in how it addresses corruption in its aid programmes. In going forward, it could increase co-ordination and joint assessments with other donors in managing risk.

Box 5.2 Germany's support to education in Mozambique – good practice in aligning project support

Despite progress towards achieving universal primary education, Mozambique faces considerable challenges: there are not enough classrooms and the quality of teaching is weak. To address these challenges, the government and donors have set up the Support Fund for the Education Sector (FASE), a pooled funding mechanism involving collaboration between eight bilateral and multilateral partners and the Ministry of Education to support Mozambique's Strategic Plan for Education.

Germany's contribution to FASE amounts to about EUR 15 million every year. In addition, Germany supports the education sector through complementary technical co-operation projects which focus on: advice to the Ministry of Education and donor co-ordination; financial planning and management, and school administration in provinces and districts; training of primary school teachers; and school constructions. Germany also supports workplace HIV programmes in the education sector, an important prevention measure to reduce teacher absenteeism due to illness. All these projects help the government to implement its strategic plan and are aligned with the government's annual programming and reporting cycle. This alignment is good practice and shows how project support can be implemented through government planning, monitoring and evaluation systems. However, Germany emphasises the importance of pooled funding in the success of this approach, providing a basis for common planning, budgeting, performance reviews and reporting among partners.

Germany has untied more ODA, including technical co-operation

Germany has made progress in untying more ODA in line with international commitments made at the high-level forums on aid effectiveness in Accra (2008) and Busan (2011). In 2013, Germany reported that 83% of its aid covered by the 2001 DAC Recommendation on untying ODA was untied, up from 78% in 2010.[4] In terms of total bilateral ODA (excluding administrative and in-donor refugees costs), the share of untied aid increased from 75% in 2010 to 80% in 2013, equalling the 2013 DAC average. Germany has also made efforts to untie its technical co-operation, the untied share of which rose from 48% in 2010 to 57% in 2013 (OECD, 2015). Germany's untying plans are to make 60% of its technical co-operation available for procurement or grants in developing countries, but this plan does not seem to cover technical co-operation from ministries other than BMZ.[5]

DAC data also indicates that foreign suppliers are in a good position to win contracts awarded by Germany – particularly suppliers from least developed countries, who won 38% of contracts in 2012 (in terms of value). This is well above the DAC average of 5% (OECD, 2014b). However, feedback from the Kenyan government suggested that Germany may reconsider how project design and procurement practices can encourage even greater use of local resources.

Conditions are transparent

Germany is transparent about the conditions it applies to its aid, and normally discusses and records any conditions during bilateral negotiations with partner governments. Germany is also committed to harmonising its conditions with those of other donors, typically through joint performance frameworks in the context of sector-wide approaches or budget support, on the basis of partner countries' development strategies and sector plans.

Germany also uses performance or results-based conditions, in which the release of funds is linked to the achievement of specific outcomes. This is the case for German support to the education sector in Mozambique but this approach raises questions (Annex C). A review of general budget support confirms that there is no clear evidence that using "variable tranches", which tend to be driven by political requirements in donor countries, generate incentives for reforms (EC, 2014). When applying such conditions, Germany should work closely with other donors to identify what measures would work best to achieve results.

Partnerships

Indicator: The member makes appropriate use of co-ordination arrangements, promotes strategic partnerships to develop synergies, and enhances mutual accountability

Germany remains committed to implementing the aid effectiveness principles, as evidenced by its active engagement with other development partners, including emerging economies through triangular co-operation. In partner countries, Germany increasingly takes a lead role in donor co-ordination and works with a range of partners who value the professionalism and expertise of its staff. While Germany is refining its strategy and tools for engaging with civil society, it remains to be seen whether its approach, including the role of Engagement Global and the use of different standards for various types of organisations, is effective.

Germany leads by example, working with other development partners through joint programming and delegated co-operation

Impressions from the visits to Kenya and Mozambique confirm that German development co-operation is widely appreciated by both partner countries and other donors. Germany is among the strongest supporters of good division of labour and joint approaches with other development partners. With most of its country programmes focusing on three to five sectors, Germany appears to be ahead of the game. In the context of the Global Partnership for Effective Development Co-operation, as co-chair since 2012, Germany is one of the driving forces behind the initiative on managing diversity and reducing fragmentation. In this context, Germany supports the exchange of experience and knowledge and promotes concrete actions for improving transparency and accountability among all development actors.[6] Within the EU, Germany is supporting joint programming efforts and is active in partner countries in promoting a clear division of labour among EU member states so as to enhance complementarity and avoid duplicating efforts.

Germany's stronger country teams allow it to play a prominent role in policy dialogue with partner governments and in co-ordinating other development partners. In Mozambique and Kenya, Germany leads on a number of sector working groups, contributing solid expertise. The embassy dedicates appropriate resources to allow Germany to engage seriously in these tasks (Annex C). Germany is also working with other donors through delegated co-operation or co-financing arrangements. In 2013, funding from other donors channelled through GIZ to complement German technical co-operation programmes worldwide amounted to EUR 177 million (GIZ, 2014),[7] and funding from other donors through co-financing arrangements with KfW amounted to EUR 340 million.[8] KfW also engages in multi-donor trust funds, particularly in countries affected by fragility and conflicts[9] and works closely with the *Agence française de développement* and the European Investment Bank through the Mutual Reliance Initiative, a platform for enhancing co-operation and division of labour.[10] Germany could look at how these arrangements lead to more effective programming and share lessons with other donors.

Germany is well placed to promote greater mutual accountability

Germany has been prominent in taking forward the international dialogue on accountability. Working closely with the UN Development Co-operation Forum in 2014,[11] BMZ helped to pin down the parameters of successful accountability, particularly in terms of bringing in a wider range of actors. This is a useful contribution for shaping effective global partnerships for the 2030 development framework. Given its leading role in co-ordinating discussion between development partners and governments in several partner countries, Germany is well placed to support efforts to establish mutual accountability mechanisms or to strengthen such processes where they exist.

Germany has lessons to share from its successful work with a range of partners, especially emerging economies

In Kenya and Mozambique, the review team saw at first-hand how Germany engages with a range of partners, all of whom value Germany's expertise. Germany has adopted strategies to work more strategically with key partners such as multilateral agencies and civil society organisations (CSOs), and is pioneering ways of engaging the private sector.

Together with Japan and Spain, Germany is among the most active DAC supporters of South-South and triangular co-operation (OECD, 2013). Germany's support to triangular co-operation is an important element of its strategy for engaging with emerging economies and regional powers (BMZ, 2011). BMZ has set up dedicated funds for triangular co-operation: one for Latin America and one for South Africa (BMZ, 2013). In addition to supporting co-operation and sharing knowledge among developing countries, Germany also plays an important role in building the capacity of emerging economies and middle-income countries as providers of development co-operation. GIZ does this through direct institutional support to development agencies in these countries and regional dialogue.[12] In order to contribute to international efforts for scaling up triangular co-operation, BMZ should consider reviewing what works well and what could be improved and share this experience with the international development community.

New strategic framework and integrated tool for working with civil society require close follow-up

BMZ values the role of civil society in development; its funding to and through non-government organisations (NGOs) has increased steadily: from USD 944 million in 2010 to USD 1 114 million in 2013, representing 8% of its total net ODA (Table B.1). In response to the 2010 peer review recommendation on its approach to civil society (Annex A), BMZ has prepared a strategy on co-operation with civil society (BMZ, 2014). A plan of action is now needed to put the strategy into practice. While BMZ puts up front the independence of civil society, some stakeholders point to a risk that the autonomy of NGOs be reduced by a tendency to use them to pursue the German government's objectives, an aspect that the plan of action should clarify.[13]

Germany gives greater autonomy in programming to political foundations and the development associations of two major churches. This differentiation with other non-state actors means that, even if political foundations and church-based organisations have to respect financial rules and comply with monitoring and auditing procedures, Germany cannot track and report in a similar way on all funding provided to German CSOs.

The way in which BMZ provides funding to non-state actors (which include single citizens, municipalities, schools and NGOs) was reorganised in 2012, merging several funding schemes into a single service point known as "Engagement Global". Fully funded by BMZ, Engagement Global employs 150 equivalent full-time staff and provides information and advisory services to these actors as well as managing funding processes (selection and monitoring of co-financed projects). Engagement Global also engages directly in development co-operation in areas such as public awareness (Chapter 6). To maximise its effectiveness and efficiency, BMZ should be clearer about Engagement Global's mandate and positioning, and look at ways to minimise its high transactions costs caused by the number of small-scale projects it selects and oversees.[14] Besides its activity-based approach which is time-consuming and fails to address capacity development properly, BMZ could consider other types of funding, such as signing multi-year framework agreements with selected entities. Having a mix of funding modalities would help BMZ to take into account the diversity of CSO roles and capacities.[15]

As noted by the review team in Mozambique and Kenya, NGOs would also appreciate more information on how to access the different funding channels. While there are good policy interactions with German NGOs at headquarters and good operational synergies with them in partner countries, field visits revealed greater scope for mutual learning through more systematic consultations in country. This would be in line with the more strategic approach envisaged in BMZ's new strategy for engaging with NGOs (BMZ, 2014).

Fragile states

Indicator: Delivery modalities and partnerships help deliver quality

Conflict sensitivity and factors exacerbating fragility are well embedded in Germany's country strategies. Germany co-ordinates actively with other development partners in international bodies on fragility; more staff may be needed to ensure that this happens systematically in the field. More flexible procedures, including an expanded range of partners and the ability to monitor programmes remotely, help to implement programmes effectively in difficult and low-capacity fragile contexts. Research is underway to learn from experiences with risk, and to develop guidance on which tools to use in different fragile contexts. Preparing country strategies through a whole-of-government approach would allow for more coherent approaches and to capitalise on links and synergies among different German actors.

Country strategies include peace and security needs, but need to bring all German ministries on board

Germany's country strategies include peace and security needs, and are based on a Peace and Conflict Assessment, and on EU joint strategy documents, where these exist. The Civil Peace Service also conducts conflict analyses and shares these with other government co-operation actors. In Kenya, the programme recognises that supporting peace is critical for development; accordingly, there is programming on corruption and transnational crime, and on alleviating religious tensions that may lead to radicalisation. Germany says that it tries to lower the technical complexity of programmes in fragile contexts; staff recognise, however, that there may be a need to be more realistic about expected results in such contexts, especially in capacity development programmes. There is also a risk of incoherence between the programmes of the different German ministries working in a given fragile state. In Kenya, for example, the country strategy covers only development programming, thereby overlooking opportunities for drawing on links and synergies with the work of other actors, including other German ministries. This could be avoided by developing whole-of-government country strategies.

Germany co-ordinates actively with other development partners

Germany works closely with international bodies on fragility, such as the International Network on Conflict and Fragility (INCAF), and in EU fragility mechanisms. The inter-ministerial guidelines on fragile states require cross-government co-ordination (FFO/MoD/BMZ, 2012) and some co-ordination groups have been set up, including for Yemen and Syria. Germany also participates in donor co-ordination forums in the field – although in Somalia the capacity to engage in these mechanisms was limited by the low level of staffing. Germany also engages with multi-donor trust funds in a range of countries, including Nepal, Liberia and South Sudan.

Germany's simplified tools and procedures in fragile contexts provide useful lessons for other donors

Germany takes a different approach in fragile contexts, using simpler, more rapid response procedures where necessary, and passing through multilateral organisations and CSOs where state capacity is weak. In Kenya, Germany also works with regional organisations on peace support programmes.[16] GIZ and KfW have a joint risk office in Nairobi, which advises on both programmatic and institutional risk, for example assessing how government devolution will affect the Kenyan programme. Remote monitoring[17] is allowed in fragile context. Programming in fragile contexts can also include loans – for example KfW has extended a loan to support the peace process in Colombia. Interestingly, Germany has commissioned a study on what policy measures and instruments are most useful in different fragile situations.[18] It is also developing a concept note on risk, based on lessons from Yemen. Germany could share the results of this research with other donors.

Notes

1. Findings from monitoring progress in meeting Busan commitments confirms that German aid could be more predictable in the medium term. While partner countries consider that information for more than two-thirds of German funds is available for one year ahead, this proportion falls to one-third when looking two years ahead (OECD/UNDP, 2014).

2. Although country strategies are primarily for internal planning, BMZ shares them with governments in partner countries as information tools.

3. BMZ adopted guidelines on the use of country systems in 2011, in line with its Busan commitments. However, these guidelines may not have been widely disseminated – country teams in Mozambique and Kenya did not refer to these guidelines during discussions with the peer review team.

4. These data reflect Germany's performance under the DAC Recommendation on Aid Untying according to the Reference Indicators Matrix (OECD, 2015). Its purpose is to monitor and assess progress made by DAC members towards more balanced effort-sharing for all untied ODA activities to the least developed and highly indebted poor countries.

5. BMZ's share of free standing technical co-operation, including activities implemented by GIZ, represents about 50% of the total free standing technical reported to the DAC. Therefore, while more than 80% of technical co-operation implemented by GIZ is untied, other ministries tie their free standing co-operation, leading to a total share of 57%.

6. At the High-Level Meeting of the Global Partnership in Mexico in 2014, Germany launched two initiatives to advance work on managing diversity and reducing fragmentation. More information is available at: http://effectivecooperation.org/wordpress/related-initiatives-2/; and www.fragmentation-diversity.org.

7. The European Commission, Australia's Department for Foreign Affairs and Trade, the Netherlands's Ministry of Foreign Affairs, and the UK Department for International Development are among those delegating the largest amounts of funds through GIZ.

8. This information is usually available in KfW annual reports, while information for 2014 was provided by KfW in handouts prepared for the DAC peer review.

9. Since 2007, KfW has engaged in 14 multi-donor trust funds, including in fragile states.

10. The Mutual Reliance Initiative, launched in 2013, provides a legally binding framework for delegating full project management and financing responsibilities to the "lead financier", using its own procedures in a way that meets the requirements of the three partners. So far, 39 projects have been co-financed.

11. The proceedings and background documents of the 2014 Germany High-Level Symposium on "Accountable and effective development co-operation in a post-2015 era" (Berlin, 20-21 March 2014) are available on the website of the UN Development Co-operation Forum at: www.un.org/en/ecosoc/newfunct/dcfgermany.shtml.

12. Examples of German support to regional dialogue includes the series of conferences at a global (https://gc21.giz.de/ibt/var/app/wp342P/1803/) and regional level (www.giz.de/en/worldwide/12942.html).

13. VENRO, the umbrella organisation for German development and humanitarian aid NGOs, sees the creation of Engagement Global as undermining the principle of subsidiarity since it took over activities previously managed by CSOs, and regrets a tendency towards using NGOs as an instrument complementing BMZ programmes – or implementing development co-operation objectives, to the detriment of their right of initiative (VENRO, 2015).

14. With a budget line of EUR 111 million, it co-financed approximately 1 000 projects in 2013 (ranging from EUR 50 000 to 500 000) and supported 6 000 volunteers.

15. More information in "Partnering with civil society – Twelve lessons from DAC peer reviews" (OECD, 2012).

16. These include the African Union and the East African Standby Force. In the latter the Ministry of Defence and the Federal Foreign Office come together in offering training in small arms and ammunition security.

17. Remote monitoring involves withdrawing or drastically reducing international and sometimes national personnel from the field, transferring greater programme responsibility to local staff or local partner organisations, and overseeing activities from a different location.

18. The German Development Institute will produce the study, due in 2015.

Bibliography

Government sources

BMZ (2014), "Strategy on government-civil society co-operation in post-2015 development policy", BMZ Strategy Paper 5/2014e, Bonn, November 2014, available at: www.bmz.de/en/publications/type_of_publication/strategies/Strategiepapier343_05_2014.pdf.

BMZ (2013), "Triangular co-operation in German development co-operation", Strategy Paper 5/2013e, Bonn and Berlin, available at: www.bmz.de/en/publications/topics/development_policy/Strategiepapier334_05_2013.pdf.

Federal Foreign Office, Federal Ministry of Defence, BMZ (2013), *For a coherent German Government Policy towards Fragile States – Inter-ministerial Guidelines.*

GIZ (2014), *Company Report 2013. GIZ. Solutions that work, Deutsche Gesellschaft für Internationale Zusammenarbeit,* Bonn, available at: www.giz.de/en/downloads/giz2014-en-annual-report-2013.pdf.

Other sources

Busan Partnership for Effective Development Co-operation (2011), endorsed at the Fourth High-Level Forum on Aid Effectiveness, Busan, Republic of Korea, 29 November - 1 December 2011, available at: http://effectivecooperation.org/.

itad (2014), "Independent Evaluation of Budget Support in Mozambique, Final Report Volume I", East Sussex, available at: www.oecd.org/derec/ec/Mz-BS-Eval-Final-Report-Vol-1.pdf.

OECD (2015), *Aid Untying: 2015 Report*, Development Assistance Committee, OECD, Paris.

OECD (2014a), Global Outlook on Aid, Results of the 2014 DAC Survey on Donors' Forward Spending Plans and Prospects, OECD, Paris, www.oecd.org/dac/aid-architecture/GlobalOutlookAid-web.pdf.

OECD (2014b), *Aid Untying: 2014 Report – Review of the Implementation of the 2001 Recommendation and the Accra and Busan Untying Commitments*, OECD, Paris.

OECD (2013), *Triangular Co-operation: What can we learn from a survey of actors involved?* OECD, Paris, available at: www.oecd.org/dac/dac-global-relations/OECD%20Triangluar%20Co-operation%20Survey%20Report%20-%20June%202013.pdf.

OECD (2012), *Partnering with civil society – Twelve lessons from DAC peer reviews*, Paris, www.oecd.org/dac/peer-reviews/12%20Lessons%20Partnering%20with%20Civil%20Society.pdf.

OECD/UNDP (2014), *Making Development Co-operation More Effective: 2014 Progress Report*, OECD Publishing, Paris, http://dx.doi.org/10.1787/9789264209305-en.

VENRO (2015), Statement, DAC peer review of Germany, VENRO, Berlin, http://venro.org/uploads/tx_igpublikationen/Statement_VENRO_DAC_2015.pdf.

Chapter 6: Results management, learning and accountability of Germany's development co-operation

Results-based management system

Indicator: A results-based management system is in place to assess performance on the basis of development priorities, objectives and systems of partner countries

BMZ has strengthened its approach to results, which is now embedded in the commissioning process with implementing agencies. A results matrix which draws on indicators and data from partner countries provides the basis for GIZ and KfW programming and reporting. This matrix helps to clarify expectations and focus attention on what programmes can realistically achieve. To finalise its approach, BMZ needs to work out how to aggregate reporting from individual activities so as to use information on results consistently for policy, planning and budgeting. In doing so, it will have a better understanding of what constitutes success and how to measure performance. Embedding the results culture within BMZ will require steering from the top.

Germany has a stronger focus on results but its approach is not yet comprehensive

Despite progress, Germany does not have a comprehensive approach to results-based management. While country strategies set the objectives for overall German development co-operation and specific programmes in each partner country (Chapter 5), it is unclear how BMZ is planning to prioritise, measure and report on results more systematically. BMZ needs to finalise its approach for aggregating reporting from individual activities, which would include adopting a set of indicators and targets against country and sector priorities. Achieving a stronger results culture within BMZ will require more steering from the top to ensure that the ministry has adequate capacity and incentives in place to shift gears.

BMZ has strengthened its approach to results at the level of individual programmes. Theapproach is now embedded in the commissioning process with implementing agencies. A results matrix, or logical framework, guides GIZ and KfW in developing new programmes and reporting on progress for each programme annually, drawing on indicators and data from national development strategies and sector plans, in line with BMZ country strategies. In general, Germany defines results in terms of outputs and outcomes and explains how achieving results at these two levels contributes to development throughout the chain of results from activities to impacts. Feedback from GIZ and KfW in Kenya and Mozambique confirmed that these results matrices help clarify expectations and focus attention on what individual programmes can realistically achieve, including during dialogue with partners. However, given the three-year project horizon for technical co-operation (Chapter 5), it is important that BMZ and GIZ work closely to break down overall longer-term results into chunks of achievements that pave the way for building capacities while addressing the longer-term perspective needed to do so in a sustainable way.

Within the DAC, Germany is among the few members pioneering how performance-based financing can deliver better results (Box 6.1). In order to prepare guidelines for taking forward its approach in this area, BMZ has taken stock of lessons. These could be of interest to other development agencies, particularly on whether and how results-based financing should influence aid delivery more broadly.

Box 6.1 Results-based financing in Kenya: improving access to health care through vouchers

German development co-operation is focusing on improving access to basic healthcare for the poor and disadvantaged groups through introducing sustainable forms of health financing. As part of its "aid on delivery" approach, KfW is subsidising healthcare vouchers to support services relating to family planning, child-birth and gender-based violence. It uses the system of vouchers to reimburse providers for delivering medical services by covering the difference between the full cost of these services and the price that beneficiaries can afford. The vouchers make it possible for poor women to acquire coupons which they can redeem against health services. So far, 300 000 poor women have benefited from better health care services through this programme.

Ii addition, the vouchers create incentives for the private sector to work in areas where public service provision is weak. The government of Kenya has been able to take advantage of the experience gained in regulating and accrediting private providers of health services as well as improving quality management to generalise the coverage of health insurance in the country. A recent review confirms that the approach is not only increasing access to services, but also the quality of services (Gorter, Ir and Meessen, 2013).

Stronger results based management would enable Germany to measure performance better and base strategic choices on experience

The absence of a results-based management system in BMZ limits the extent to which Germany can define success and measure its overall performance in supporting partner countries to achieve their own development priorities. In the absence of overall indicators and targets, it is unclear how BMZ is using results information from programme implementation and other sources of evidence to feed into strategic planning and public communication.

GIZ and KfW use results information routinely for improving overall programme management. Both organisations have good monitoring systems in place, drawing primarily on indicators and data from partner countries' own systems, which limits the need for additional monitoring and reporting requirements. In addition, most technical co-operation programmes include a specific component for strengthening partner countries' monitoring and evaluation systems. The review team saw at first hand during the visits to Kenya and Mozambique how German development co-operation puts this approach into practice (Annex C).

Like other donors, Germany could strengthen the credibility of its reporting on results by better explaining what drives outcomes and impacts in the context of wider development processes. In moving forward on measuring results, BMZ will need to make a distinction between different levels of results in order to be able to establish the link between activities financed by German development co-operation and their impact on development in partner countries. Results matrices from individual programmes provide a good basis to support meaningful analysis throughout the results chain from activities to impact. Although implementing agencies apply rigorous impact measurement methodologies only in selected cases, they tend to report on results not only at the level of outputs but also on outcomes and impacts based on a contribution analysis. However, when it comes to communicating results to the public, GIZ and KfW report mainly on outputs such as the numbers of people having improved access to water and sanitation facilities, a measure which does not capture the impact in improving hygiene and health outcomes.[1]

The approach to results in fragile contexts is pragmatic

Results setting in fragile contexts is realistic, based on a solid analysis of the conflict and related risks, and taking into account principles such as do no harm. Remote monitoring is permitted in fragile contexts. Such remote monitoring means that Germany can monitor a partner's programme using third parties, usually because donor staff are unable to access the programme site due to security constraints.

Evaluation system

Indicator: The evaluation system is in line with the DAC evaluation principles

Important changes have taken place in Germany's approach to evidence, learning and accountability. BMZ has allocated more resources for evaluation, notably with the creation of the German Institute for Development Evaluation (DEval), but still needs to ensure that evaluation plans focus on addressing strategic priorities and risks. Realising DEval's potential will require strong leadership, strategic planning, adequate funding and independent reporting lines. While GIZ and KfW both have reinforced their independent evaluation of individual projects, the link between evaluations and results frameworks is not yet in place.

Germany has increased focus on evaluation

As recommended by the 2010 peer review (Annex A), BMZ has allocated more resources for evaluation. In 2012 it created the German Institute for Development Evaluation (DEval), a separate public entity owned by the Federal Government.[2] In addition to evaluating and measuring the impact of German development co-operation focussing on strategic issues, the new institute aims to provide methodological support to improve the quality of evaluation and ensure that lessons from evaluation can improve future co-operation. DEval's mandate is in line with the *DAC Principles for Evaluation of Development Assistance* (OECD, 1991).

In order to ensure that DEval can deliver its mandate with full impartiality and independence, BMZ may need to reflect further about the governance of this new entity, including the role of its advisory board[3] and reporting lines to the government. BMZ has control over DEval in terms of budget, procedures and organisation. Moreover, the ministry approves DEval's multi-annual evaluation plan and is responsible for submitting evaluation reports to Parliament. With the creation of DEval, BMZ may also need to review its own evaluation policy and clarify its role vis-à-vis strategic evaluation.[4]

To complement Deval's strategic level evaluation, GIZ[5] and KfW[6] have their own plans, budgets and teams for project-level evaluations focusing on learning. Their policies and guidelines are in line with DAC principles and standards. Notably, their evaluation structures are independent of the departments responsible for managing programmes and report directly to their respective organisation's management boards.

The review team was not able to identify the extent to which other ministries with growing aid budgets evaluate their activities routinely.[7] As part of its overall oversight role, BMZ could do more to share its evaluation culture and methodology across other parts of the government.

Evaluation lacks strategic focus

Strengthening the strategic focus of Germany's evaluation is long overdue, having been noted by previous DAC peer reviews. While the various evaluation systems seem to have adequate resources, a more strategic approach is needed so that Germany can get the most out of its evaluations. Setting up an evaluation plan should be based on a clear understanding of what needs to be learned across the various programmes and institutions, especially for results management.

It is too early to say if the creation of DEval will help BMZ to drive its overall programme more strategically. In its first two years of existence, DEval has struggled with leadership[8] and so far, it has completed only a couple of evaluations. The review team also noted in Kenya and Mozambique that while implementing agencies evaluate projects routinely, German development co-operation could benefit from a more strategic approach (Annex C). This could include periodic portfolio reviews for providing the evidence base for

BMZ to make future strategic choices, as is the case for development co-operation in fragile states.

Germany is active in strengthening the evaluation capacity of partner countries

In line with its commitment to support greater leadership by partner countries, Germany supports international efforts to strengthen the capacity of partner countries to evaluate their own policies and programmes, including in the context of the Task Team on Evaluation Capacity Development of the DAC Network on Development Evaluation. Most GIZ programmes include a component for strengthening monitoring and evaluation systems. BMZ also works closely with developing country partners when evaluating its programmes by establishing "a reference group for the South" for each evaluation, a group responsible for advising on the evaluation throughout the process. Despite these notable efforts, Germany has yet to consider how it could rely more on evaluations conducted by partner countries when managing their own policies and programmes.

Institutional learning

Indicator: Evaluations and appropriate knowledge management systems are used as management tools

The overall coherence and efficiency of Germany's approach to knowledge management needs to be consolidated. While implementing agencies have systems in place to disseminate evaluation findings and share experience, BMZ needs to ensure that it manages and uses this knowledge both centrally and through implementing agencies, and make evidence available systematically, including for staff seconded to embassies in developing countries.

Systems are in place for learning from evaluation

In order to integrate evaluation findings into decision making, BMZ's evaluation unit together with operational departments draw a plan indicating how they will act upon the management response. In addition, the evaluation unit is responsible for reviewing how this plan is implemented after 12 to 18 months, reporting to senior management in the ministry. Such a system will give more weight to the management response which has now become mandatory. Both GIZ and KfW have also increased the focus on learning through mechanisms to use and disseminate evaluation findings within their own organisations. KfW publishes a biennial report which analyses the results of all evaluations carried out over a period of two years. The last such publication focused on how to bring sustainable improvements in fragile states (KfW, 2013). KfW also carries out analysis of specific themes, using data available from its *ex-post* evaluation reports.[9] Every two years GIZ prepares a report on the findings of monitoring and evaluations. The latest report revealed its programmes to be highly relevant, but there were sustainability challenges (GIZ, 2013b). GIZ also prepares studies on specific themes to learn from experiences across a range of programmes, drawing on findings from various evaluations, reviews and progress reports. GIZ has also introduced a management response for strengthening follow-up on recommendations from evaluations.

Knowledge management is an on-going process within GIZ and KfW

The implementing agencies have introduced several mechanisms for improving how they use knowledge to improve future planning and decision-making although they may need to build stronger incentives to encourage staff to prioritise learning. Both GIZ and KfW have created incentives for reinforcing the evaluation culture within their respective organisations. Examples include "swapping" roles, whereby evaluation departments borrow staff from operational departments, a process which helps to consolidate mutual learning.

In line with its strong identity as a learning organisation, GIZ is continuously improving its approach to learning, guided by a strategy (GIZ, 2013a). Following the merger of the various technical co-operation agencies (Chapter 5), GIZ has revamped its information technology solutions and platforms which now allow for strong virtual collaboration and e-learning within and across regional and sector teams. KfW has a dedicated network to take regular stock of progress and launch new initiatives. The reorganisation of KfW (Chapter 5) has introduced "centres of excellence" to review, analyse and disseminate information, including findings from evaluations, on relevant sectors and themes across the organisation.

The review team noted during the visits to Mozambique and Kenya that learning works well within individual agencies and programmes. However, it is unclear how BMZ brings together the various parts of the system to make full use of knowledge generated at different levels, including research from universities and think thanks such as the German Development Institute. In particular, it may want to reflect on whether a more comprehensive approach to country teams, i.e. without distinguishing between headquarters and country level, would help to make the relevant information available more systematically, particularly to staff posted in embassies in partner countries.

Communication, accountability and development awareness

Indicator: The member communicates development results transparently and honestly

Germany has increased its public information on individual projects through a dedicated web-based transparency portal. This is in line with international commitments on transparency. Although BMZ uses a range of different communication tools, it is not yet able to aggregate reporting from individual activities into an overall narrative describing whether or not development co-operation is successful. BMZ could build on the experience of launching the Charter for the Future to step up its communication efforts.

Germany is making good progress towards its transparency commitments

Germany has taken action to increase the publicly available information on development co-operation, in line with commitments made in Busan in 2011. BMZ now publishes data to the registry of the International Aid Transparency Initiative (IATI), focusing on BMZ-funded projects implemented by GIZ and KfW (IATI, 2014).[10] BMZ updates the information on its website every six months and plans to increase this to every three months in the future.[11] Information is not systematically available in the language of partner countries, however, which limits accessibility. BMZ reporting now also includes government funds channelled through German NGOs, but has yet to include funding through multilateral organisations. Other federal ministries which are responsible for growing aid budgets, particularly the Federal Foreign Office and the Ministry for Environment, have yet to adopt their own transparency plans or provide more information on what they are doing. To comply with the Busan common, open standard on transparency by 2015,[12] Germany will need to publish more detailed information which meets information needs of developing countries, including on results achieved and forward-looking spending, and to ensure that all parts of the government are transparent about their action.

Germany's commitment to transparency also translates into its international action on climate finance: BMZ and the Ministry for Environment publish information on German climate finance online (Chapter 1) and support international efforts to increase the transparency of climate change finance in the context of the UNFCCC.

Germany needs to tell a more compelling story of its development achievements

As Germany celebrates the "European Year of Development" in 2015 and plays a lead role internationally in chairing the G7, BMZ could adopt a more systematic approach to communication, targeting specific audiences with relevant messages about the achievements of German development co-operation. BMZ uses a range of communication tools, but does not appear to bring these tools together to get the most out of its efforts to raise public awareness of development. In order to be able to tell a compelling story of what success looks like, and inform debates on the impacts of German development co-operation and the risks involved, BMZ needs to consolidate its results-based management system. BMZ could also step up communication efforts, building on the momentum and public goodwill and interest which emerged when launching the Charter for the Future.

Germany is prioritising awareness raising

Germany continues to benefit from strong public support for aid. The latest EU poll (EC, 2015) shows that 46% of the German public consider that it is "very important" to help people in developing countries, while 45% consider such action as "fairly important". Such strong support stems partly from BMZ's investment in development education. With a budget of EUR 23 million in 2014, BMZ has doubled its funding in this area since 2010. Engagement Global (Chapter 5) is responsible for managing this funding, targeting primarily school children and university students to increase their interest in sustainable development and global challenges.

Notes

1. Information provided in factsheets produced by the German embassy in Kenya: www.nairobi.diplo.de/Vertretung/nairobi/en/005 Development 20Cooperation/s Water Sanitation.html.

2. With an annual budget of EUR 7 million and 48 staff, DEval mainly carries out evaluations itself, rather than using external experts.

3. DEval's advisory board is made up of representatives from all parliamentary groups in the German Parliament as well as from GIZ, KfW, the churches and political foundations, and NGOs and academia. This body advises the institute on how best to perform its role, focusing in particular on the evaluation programme and lessons learned from evaluations, but seems to have little to say in overall DEval's strategic orientation.

4. It has retained a budget of EUR 1.5 million and employs 5.5 staff to oversee DEval's work and participate in joint evaluations with other donors.

5. GIZ conducts about 100 project evaluations every year. Since 2014, evaluations have been compulsory for all technical co-operation projects over EUR 1 million and a duration of minimum three years and are part of project budgets. GIZ also has an annual budget of EUR 500 000 to conduct three to five corporate strategy evaluations every year on the basis of a two-year programme.

6. KfW has an annual budget of EUR 3 million for evaluation and employs 11 staff. It evaluates a representative sample of 50% of all completed projects, which translates into around 50 *ex post* evaluations every year. It also conducts impact evaluations on selective themes.

7. BMZ and the Federal Foreign Office have conducted a joint evaluation of German humanitarian assistance (FFO and BMZ, 2012). Their findings were used to inform the Federal Foreign Office's strategy and new approaches to its humanitarian programme.

8. Despite reference to German development co-operation as a whole, DEval supports primarily BMZ and its implementing organisations, especially GIZ and KfW, as well as NGOs. BMZ appointed a new director in April 2015 after a long period of acting arrangements involving a senior staff from the ministry.

9. For example, KfW recently conducted a systematic review of how financial co-operation affects employment generation (KfW, 2015).

10. BMZ launched its IATI data-driven portal in 2014 (www.bmz.de/de/was wir machen/wege/transparenz-fuer-mehr-Wirksamkeit/iati/index.jsp). Both GIZ and KfW have their own portals which provide some basic information on their activities and give access to some project-related documents.

11. Although BMZ has expanded its reporting – which now includes new information fields, such as project description, implementing partners, commitment dates, sectors, and terms and conditions – it does not specify a timeline for publishing forward-looking activity budgets, information on results and project documents.

12. Stakeholders in Busan resolved to make information on development co-operation and other development resources better available and publicly accessible. They set out to implement a common, open standard for electronic publication of timely, comprehensive and forward-looking information on resources for development co-operation by the end of 2015. See: www.oecd.org/development/aid-architecture/acommonstandard.htm.

Bibliography

Government sources

FFO and BMZ (2012), *Joint Evaluation German Humanitarian Aid Abroad,* Federal Foreign Office and BMZ, Berlin.

GIZ (2013a), *Learning from Evaluations: Processes and instruments used by GIZ as a learning organisation and their contribution to inter-organisational learning,* GIZ, Bonn and Eschborn.

GIZ (2013b), *Measuring – Assessing – Making Improvements, Findings and conclusions from monitoring and evaluation, 2010-2012*, GIZ, Bonn and Eschborn.

KfW (2015), "Employment effects of financial co-operation: an estimation model", KfW Position Paper, January 2015, Frankfurt, available at: www.kfw-entwicklungsbank.de/PDF/Download-Center/PDF-Dokumente-Positionspapiere/2015_01_22_PP_-Besch%C3%A4ftigungsmodell_EN.pdf.

KfW (2013), *Fragile Settings. Lasting Impact*, 12th Evaluation Report on Projects and Programmes in Developing Countries 2011-2012, KfW Development Bank, Frankfurt.

Other sources

European Commission (2015), The European Year for Development – Citizens' Views on Development, Co-operation and Aid, Special Eurobarometer 421, Brussels, January 2015.

Gorter, A.C., P. Ir and B. Meessen (2013), *Results-Based Financing of Maternal and Newborn Health Care in Low- and Lower-middle-Income Countries*, Evidence Review, study commissioned and funded by BMZ through the GIZ project PROFILE, Bonn and Eschborn, available at www.oecd.org/dac/peer-reviews/Evidence-RBF-maternal-health.pdf.

IATI (2014), *Annual Report 2014*, report available online at: www.aidtransparency.net/reports/IATI-annual-report-2014.pdf.

OECD (1991), *DAC Principles for Evaluation of Development Assistance*, OECD, Paris, available at: www.oecd.org/development/evaluation/2755284.pdf.

Chapter 7: Germany's humanitarian assistance

Strategic framework

Indicator: Clear political directives and strategies for resilience, response and recovery

In Germany humanitarian assistance sits within the Federal Foreign Office; this is complemented by BMZ's development and transitional aid; and BMZ's special initiatives, which, at least in part, deal with the causes of, and fall-out from, humanitarian crises. There is a renewed political commitment in the German government to humanitarian aid through the coalition agreement. The Foreign Office has a new, strategic approach to humanitarian aid, covering both response and preparedness, an area where Germany is making significant efforts, both through its programming and on the global stage. The lack of clarity of BMZ's transition strategy is limiting Germany's ability to systematically support holistic responses in protracted crises and transition situations; the peer review team has been told that there are plans to redesign this area of the programme; this is welcomed. There is also scope for an increased budget share for humanitarian programming.

There is political commitment for humanitarian aid and a clear strategic approach from the Foreign Office – but BMZ's transition strategy is still unclear

The Federal Foreign Office has a new strategic approach to humanitarian assistance, building on broad consultation with partners, both in Germany and in the field (FFO, 2012). This represents good progress towards the recommendations of the 2010 peer review (OECD, 2011) and the 2012 joint evaluation of German humanitarian aid (FFO/BMZ, 2012). The strategy applies the principles of Good Humanitarian Donorship (GHD, 2003) and the EU Consensus on Humanitarian Aid (EU, 2008), and sets out clear good practice objectives for programming; these will eventually be complemented by regional, country, and sector strategies (FFO, 2012). Political commitments for humanitarian assistance are also included in the Coalition Agreement, including the desire to place more emphasis on humanitarian aid, and to seek political solutions to humanitarian crises (CDU, CSU and SPD, 2013).

If Germany is to provide a truly holistic response to humanitarian crises, the Federal Foreign Office's humanitarian aid needs to be complemented by BMZ's transitional aid. BMZ's transition strategy states that, "The overarching aim of transitional development assistance is to increase the resilience of people and institutions to withstand the impact and consequences of crises, violent conflict and extreme natural events while improving the prospects for sustainable development" (BMZ, 2013). It covers the areas set out in the division of labour agreed between BMZ and the Federal Foreign Office (Box 7.1). However, the strategy lacks clarity by not setting out clearly the tools and partnerships it will rely on, making it difficult to see how Germany will deliver on this part of the humanitarian programme. Germany has informed the peer review team of plans to redesign this area of the programme, which is welcomed.

Unclear access to recovery finance is hindering holistic responses

The 2010 peer review found that links between humanitarian and development programming were unclear, a finding echoed by the 2012 joint evaluation (FFO/BMZ, 2012). In 2011, the Federal Foreign Office and BMZ agreed on a division of labour (Box 7.1), in which BMZ was responsible for recovery and rehabilitation, longer-term food security, the reintegration of refugees and displaced people, and the reconstruction of basic social and economic infrastructure (FFO/BMZ, 2011). However, partners are confused about how BMZ is implementing this mandate, and whether (and how) there is funding available for this type of work. NGOs applying for recovery funds have been passed on to BMZ's NGO programme (Chapter 5.2), while others who would be natural partners for refugee reintegration programmes have been turned away completely. The peer review team also heard how the drought response in Kenya in 2011 could have been more effective and sustainable if responses had been longer-term, rather than just alleviating immediate symptoms; however, no funding for this type of work was available at that time. However, in 2013 a drought resilience programme focusing on the affected regions became part of bilateral development co-operation (Box 7.2).

Box 7.1 The humanitarian division of labour between BMZ and the Federal Foreign Office

Germany has attempted to clarify the division of labour between BMZ and the Federal Foreign Office through an inter-ministerial agreement signed in November 2011 and entering into force in May 2012.

Under the division of labour, the Federal Foreign Office is responsible for:

- Immediate emergency assistance following natural disasters or political conflicts
- Ongoing emergency assistance in longer-term crises, especially complex crises
- Humanitarian transitional assistance to complement emergency assistance
- Disaster reduction and risk management, including preparedness measures
- Humanitarian mine and ordnance clearance
- Measures aimed at strengthening the international humanitarian assistance system.

BMZ is responsible for:

- Disaster risk management
- Medium to long-term food security for people caught up in crises, disasters and conflicts, including the relationship with the World Food Programme
- Reintegration of refugees and internally displaced persons in the context of crises, disasters and conflicts
- Reconstruction of basic social and economic infrastructure.

Source: FFO/BMZ (2011)

Preparedness is a key focus of Foreign Office programming

The Foreign Office has included preparedness as part of its core strategy, including capacity building for national and local crisis structures, and to improve the preparedness capacity of German NGOs. The Foreign Office has also been very active in lobbying for preparedness on the global stage; hosting a multi-stakeholder conference in June 2013, which led to the Principles and Recommendations on Preparedness.[1] To complement emergency assistance, BMZ's Special Initiative One World, No Hunger (Chapter 2) stresses the need to enhance resilience to prevent famine; this will no doubt also be useful once put into practice. BMZ is also in the middle of a Resilience Learning Initiative[2] to support its transition strategy (BMZ, 2013).

The humanitarian budget share could continue to grow

The 2015 humanitarian budget is expected to be around EUR 420 million (BMZ, 2015), up from EUR 283 million in 2008. This meets the 2010 peer review recommendation to increase humanitarian spending. However, it still only represents 6.5% of budgeted German ODA;[3] 15 DAC members allocate more than 7% for humanitarian programming, with 10 of these allocating more than 10% of their total ODA.[4] This clearly leaves scope for further budgetary effort.

Effective programme design

Indicator: Programmes target the highest risk to life and livelihood

There has been significant improvement in the Federal Foreign Office's humanitarian programming, which is now focused on areas where Germany can clearly add value and on quality partnerships. There are also systems in place to ensure that early warning leads to early action; this has proved useful in sudden onset crises, such as the Kenyan drought. The Foreign Office actively promotes the participation of affected people in its partners' programmes; this is good practice. However, there is a lack of clarity over BMZ's tools for transitional assistance and the Special Initiatives, hampering a consistent German approach to humanitarian situations.

The Foreign Office's programme is correctly focused on comparative advantage and quality partners; but more clarity about the wider humanitarian approach would be useful

The 2012 joint evaluation found that Germany's humanitarian aid was fragmented, and recommended that Germany focus on areas where it has comparative advantage, competence and experience (FFO/BMZ, 2012). The Federal Foreign Office has worked hard to implement this recommendation by:

- developing country and sector strategies – including for selected forgotten crises – that outline policy and funding intentions, in consultation with the Humanitarian Aid Co-ordinating Committee;
- adding value to its funding decisions, for example by hosting the Berlin Conference on the Syrian Refugee Situation;[5]
- applying strict quality criteria when choosing partners, including their capacity to respond, both overall and in particular crises, and their ability to implement a holistic response – from relief to recovery;
- withdrawing from crisis situations where there is no clear added value, such as Latin America, and ceasing funding partners failing to meet the quality criteria.

Partners agree that the Foreign Office's decision-making process is transparent and matches its strategic orientations. The peer review team also heard that field staff, including in Somalia, have input into funding proposals and send assessment information back to Berlin. This process of incorporating on-the-ground reality in decision making is good practice.

BMZ's funding criteria are less clear, and the division of labour – especially in areas where both the Foreign Office and BMZ have retained a role – has led to confusion about the focus of Germany's overall humanitarian effort (Box 7.1). For example, BMZ told the peer review team that it only funds large programmes – EUR 1 million and up – and focuses on areas outlined in the division of labour (food security, infrastructure, assistance to refugees and host community disaster risk management), but was less clear on how it decides where and who to fund[6]. In addition, partners highlighted that food security is covered by both institutions. Avoiding confusion in the funding of food security has required creative efforts, as German budget rules do not allow for joint financing – so the Foreign Office and BMZ have to agree on which projects each will fund on a case by case basis. In Somalia, where both BMZ and the Foreign Office provide funds, the split is geographical with the Foreign Office funding partners in the South Central area, and BMZ funding the North; while this does prevent overlap between the institutions, it does not help create a holistic set of German criteria for the Somalia response.

Early warning for early action

Germany uses its own channels – primarily field missions – to monitor potential crisis situations, and feed this information back to Berlin. Partners agree that this has led to early funding decisions, for example on Syria and Ukraine, and for the drought crisis in Kenya (Box 7.2).

Affected people are involved in programmes

The participation of affected people in programme design, implementation and monitoring is a critical part of effective humanitarian assistance; the Federal Foreign Office asks partners to integrate this perspective into their programming. It also provides funding for partners to improve their capacity in this area, including adhering to the Humanitarian Accountability Partnership Standard in Accountability and Quality Management;[7] this is good practice. There are other examples of German work in this area; in Kenya, GIZ placed an expert inside Transparency International Kenya to develop a one-stop complaints mechanism for humanitarian aid, building on a similar GIZ Kenya project on corruption.

Box 7.2 Development funding for drought response in Kenya

The response to the 2011 drought emergency in northern Kenya demonstrates Germany's capacity to create holistic, phased responses, bringing together a range of humanitarian and development instruments. The initial emergency response involved providing short-term funding – from both the Federal Foreign Office and BMZ – to NGOs, the World Food Programme and GIZ, who focused on alleviating immediate food insecurity and water issues in the areas affected by the drought. This was followed by a call for proposals for the medium-term response – up to one year – including projects for livestock restocking, drought-resistant seed, and water supply. The third phase involved supporting the Kenyan government's development objective of Ending Drought Emergency[8] as part of GIZ's ongoing development programming.

Source: Peer review team discussions with German staff and partners in Kenya.

Effective delivery, partnerships and instruments

Indicator: Delivery modalities and partnerships help deliver quality assistance

The Federal Foreign Office has the right tools and supportive, strategic partnerships for an effective response in both rapid onset crises and complex emergencies. Germany is also serious about co-ordination with other donors, both on global policy issues and in the field. However, Germany's recovery funding needs to be more predictable and less complicated to access.

Germany has the right tools for complex emergencies, but recovery funding is unpredictable

The Foreign Office has the right tools for supporting a comprehensive approach to complex crises. Restrictions on eligible expenditure have been removed, and the Foreign Office can now support capacity building – critical, for example, for its preparedness mandate – and more modern approaches such as cash programming and pooled funding. The high levels of earmarking noted by the joint evaluation are gone; partners agree that the trend towards larger grants over a longer period has provided the necessary predictability to develop more strategic approaches to crisis response. There is also a trend towards multi-annual funding, up to 36 months for UN partners and 24 months for NGO interventions, for example in Yemen. The Foreign Office now has budget predictability and a solid strategic approach to humanitarian assistance; this provides the right foundations to provide more of its funding on a multi-annual basis.

BMZ provides its recovery and rehabilitation funding via the standard NGO call for proposal process (Chapter 5); approval takes between four to six months. This means that partners have no predictability about whether they will receive recovery support to follow on from their emergency interventions. The special initiatives also provide funds for some humanitarian situations, such as to support new refugee inflows to Kakuma camp in Kenya, and to support returns and host communities in Kismayo. Although commitments can be multi-annual, funds must be disbursed according to a fixed timeline, which limits the scope and sustainability of recovery programmes.

Germany's rapid response and civil protection tools are universally praised

Partners universally praise the Foreign Office's rapid response funding, noting that it is quick – decisions are made within hours or days – and that procedures are uncomplicated. Germany has also shown that it can divert development funding for new emergencies (Box 7.2). Partner funding can be complemented by civil protection responses through the Federal Agency for Technical Relief (known by its German acronym, THW), including search and rescue capacity, mobile water purification and technical and logistics support to UN agencies, including the World Food Programme and the UN's refugee agency (UNHCR).[9] Embassies can also access some Foreign Office funds for use in smaller crises.

Partnerships are supportive and strategic; but recovery funds are cumbersome to access

The Foreign Office has adopted a "three-pillar" approach to partnerships, meaning that it engages with three sets of partners: United Nations actors, the Red Cross movement and NGOs. Partnerships have all become more strategic by reducing earmarking and by promoting regular policy dialogue, both bilaterally, but also through the Humanitarian Aid Co-ordinating Committee, where the NGO platform, VENRO, is the rotating chair. The Foreign Office also helps NGOs to professionalise, for example by helping them integrate accountability standards and financially supporting their engagement in international policy debates.[10] In the field, German partners (including GIZ) are brought together to share information on specific issues. Partners in Kenya would like this to be more systematic to ensure coherency and synergy between German efforts at different layers of society.

The 2010 peer review asked Germany to provide a uniform proposal and reporting system for humanitarian and recovery funding to decrease the transaction costs of dealing with two institutions. This has not yet been done. While partners agree that the Foreign Office's administrative burden is appropriate, they question whether BMZ's heavy bureaucracy and complicated set of entry points are appropriate for humanitarian contexts.

Germany is serious about co-ordination with other donors

Germany takes its role as a major humanitarian donor seriously, with the Foreign Office co-chairing both the Good Humanitarian Donorship initiative in 2011-12, where it focused on preparedness; and the OCHA donor support group,[11] where it promoted outreach to newer donors. It also regularly participates in European donor co-ordination through the Committee on Humanitarian Aid and Food Aid. Germany also participates in donor groups in the field, including an informal group on Somalia (Annex C).

Organisation fit for purpose

Indicator: Systems, structures, processes and people work together effectively and efficiently

There is good strategic co-ordination among Germany's actors – including NGOs and the various parts of government involved in humanitarian response. Germany is also raising awareness of civil military principles, both with its own military and with other nations' peacekeeping forces. Staff in the field, and in Berlin, are seen as knowledgeable on humanitarian issues. A range of good practice innovations, such as staff exchanges with humanitarian agencies, have been developed.

Co-ordination of humanitarian actors is effective and strategic

The 2010 peer review asked Germany to clarify the division of labour between the Foreign Office and BMZ; the inter-ministerial agreement is a good step towards this (Box 7.1), although some areas of duplication remain, such as disaster risk reduction and food aid. Both parties are attempting to abide by the provisions of this agreement. Co-ordination across government and with other German actors takes place through the Humanitarian Aid Co-ordinating Committee, which regularly brings together German NGOs, the Red Cross and United Nations agencies, BMZ, the Foreign Office, and the Ministries of Defence and Interior to discuss overall strategy, plus major issues such as Ebola and Syria. This is widely seen as a useful tool.

Civil-military links are principled and constructive

Germany works to increase awareness of humanitarian principles amongst military personnel. A joint paper prepared by the German military and the NGO platform, VENRO, on civil-military co-ordination, recognises the need to separate military and humanitarian funding and operations, while supporting constructive dialogue. In Kenya, the peer review team heard about GIZ's project to train peacekeepers at the International Peace Support Training Centre (in Nairobi) on civil-military issues; this is good practice.

Knowledgeable staff in Berlin and in the field

Partners have frank and open discussions with Federal Foreign Office staff, whom they find knowledgeable on humanitarian issues. The Foreign Office encourages efforts to build staff skills; there are regular staff exchanges with OCHA, other United Nations agencies and the German Red Cross, and regional trainings on humanitarian issues for field based staff. BMZ's restructuring and subsequent staff turnover has meant that partners have had to re-establish relationships; no doubt this will settle down with time.

Results, learning and accountability

Indicator: Results are measured and communicated, and lessons learnt

The findings of the useful joint evaluation of the humanitarian programme in 2012 have been integrated into the Federal Foreign Office's strategy and programme approaches. Partner reporting is focused on results and lessons; field staff are also involved in monitoring where security conditions permit. However, there are no indicators to monitor Germany's own progress towards good humanitarian donorship. In addition, Germany could make better use of partners' communications materials.

More effort needed on monitoring

The findings of the joint BMZ/Foreign Office evaluation of the German humanitarian programme in 2012 (BMZ/FFO 2012) have clearly been useful in stimulating the division of labour and in improving the quality of the Foreign Office's programming. This evaluation could be followed up with regular monitoring, which will require developing indicators to monitor Germany's progress towards good humanitarian donorship.

An increased focus on partner results, and on field monitoring where possible

The joint evaluation recommended that Germany introduce results-oriented reporting by partners (FFO/BMZ, 2012); partners report that this has been done. The Federal Foreign Office's humanitarian strategy talks about the need for regular evaluations (FFO, 2012), and there is an understanding that this should be done in a way that is relevant to humanitarian operations and promotes learning. Regular monitoring is left to field staff, who travel to review projects when security permits. In Somalia, where access is limited, field staff will also rely on the monitoring of other donors. There are plans to discuss more effective monitoring tools, including possibilities for "remote control" monitoring, in the donor group.

Making better use of partner communications materials

There is a four-yearly report on humanitarian results that is fed back to parliament. Partners in the field report that they send communications materials, such as YouTube videos, photos and anecdotal stories to Germany, but that this is on an ad hoc basis; the Foreign Office and BMZ could make better use of these materials for their communication.

Notes

1. Available at: www.preventionweb.net/files/33663_33663conferenceondisaterpreparednes.pdf.
2. BMZ has invited its implementing partners to become part of a facilitated Learning Initiative looking at how strengthening resilience can be effectively realised in project planning and implementation; how to define "success" when addressing the topic of resilience in programming; and how to measure resilience.
3. Based on the 2015 budget ODA figure of EUR 6.44 billion.
4. Canada, Finland, Ireland, Italy, Luxembourg, Norway, Sweden, Switzerland, the United Kingdom and the United States all allocated more than 10% of their ODA to humanitarian assistance in 2012.
5. The conference was hosted by Foreign Minister Frank-Walter Steinmeier, Federal Minister for Economic Co-operation and Development Gerd Müller and UN High Commissioner for Refugees António Guterres on 28 October 2014. It was attended by representatives of around 40 countries and international organisations. More at: www.auswaertigesamt.de/EN/Aussenpolitik/RegionaleSchwerpunkte/NaherMittlererOsten/syriarefugeeconference/Uebersicht_node.htm.
6. BMZ later informed the review team that there is a list of 10 countries eligible for transitional assistance funding and that a set of quality criteria, including a resilience marker, is used to inform spending decisions.
7. See: www.hapinternational.org.
8. The Government of Kenya has made a commitment to end the worst of the suffering caused by drought by 2022. The actions needed to achieve this are set out in the Drought Risk Management and Ending Drought Emergencies Medium Term Plan (MTP) for 2013-17, which is part of the Kenya Vision 2030 MTP2. More at: www.dmikenya.or.ke/home/18-newitem/34-drm-and-ede-common-programming-process.html .
9. For more on THW's work in international crisis response see: www.thw.de/EN/Homepage/homepage_node.html.
10. German NGOs note that thanks to German funding they have been able to engage with the Global cluster leads, with the Inter Agency Standing Committee and its Humanitarian Financing Task Team, and with the UN Office for the Co-ordination of Humanitarian Affairs (OCHA) Country-based Pooled Funding dialogue.
11. Germany was co-chair of the OCHA Donor Support Group in 2012-13.

Bibliography

Government sources

BMZ (2013), "Strategy on transitional development assistance: strengthening resilience – Shaping Transition", BMZ Strategy Paper 6/2013e, BMZ, Bonn, available at: https://www.bmz.de/en/publications/type_of_publication/strategies/Strategiepapier335_06_2013.pdf.

BMZ (2015), *OECD DAC Peer Review of Germany 2015 – Memorandum by Germany*, BMZ, Bonn.

CDU/CSU/SPD (2013), *Shaping Germany's Future – Coalition treaty between CDU/CSU and SPD, 18th legislative period*, unofficial translation, available at: www.kas.de/wf/doc/kas_36853-544-2-30.pdf?140820093605.

FFO (2012), *Strategy of the Federal Foreign Office for Humanitarian Assistance Abroad*, FFO, Berlin.

FFO and BMZ (2011), *Guide outlining the tasks of the Federal Foreign Office and The Federal Ministry for Economic Co-operation and Development in the Spheres of Humanitarian Assistance as well as Recovery and Rehabilitation,* FFO and BMZ, Berlin.

FFO and BMZ (2012), *Joint Evaluation of German Humanitarian Aid Abroad,* Federal Foreign Office and BMZ, Berlin.

Other sources

EU (2008), *The European Consensus on Humanitarian Aid,* European Union, Brussels, available at: http://ec.europa.eu/echo/files/media/publications/consensus_en.pdf.

Good Humanitarian Donorship (2003), *The Principles and Good Practice of Humanitarian Donorship,* agreement signed in Stockholm, available at: http://www.ghdinitiative.org/.

OECD (2011), *OECD Development Assistance Peer Reviews: Germany 2010*, OECD Publishing, Paris, available at: http://dx.doi.org/10.1787/9789264098299-en.

Annex A: Progress since the 2010 DAC peer review recommendations

Key issues: development beyond aid

Recommendations 2010	Progress on implementation
Continue to provide international leadership on climate change approaches and fulfil international commitments, particularly to "fast start" financing for climate change mitigation and adaptation and for REDD+.	**Implemented**
Establish an overarching policy statement on policy coherence for development and a clearly prioritised coherence agenda which sets strategic cross-governmental goals and provides a clear plan for implementation.	**Partially implemented**
Determine where responsibility for co-ordinating whole of government approaches sits within government, ensuring that sufficient capacity for analysis and strategy development resides in the responsible entity, as well as instil a sound development perspective within relevant ministries' policies.	**Partially implemented**

Key issues: strategic orientations

Recommendations 2010	Progress on implementation
Publish a clearly-defined overarching policy for development co-operation that drives forward progress on the MDGs and poverty reduction, paying particular attention to conflict and fragility and to sub-Saharan Africa, and that further concentrates Germany's aid.	**Implemented**
Base its draft strategy for multilateral aid on a clear analysis of how its development objectives could be advanced through multilateral funding, while also taking into account Germany's specific objectives for influencing and reforming multilateral institutions, resource allocation and collaboration with other partners to make multilateral aid more effective.	**Implemented**

Develop its private sector programme to encourage foreign and domestic investments in areas aligned to partner countries' development strategies, ensuring that this does not lead it to divert ODA to finance assistance that is oriented to its own commercial interests.	**Implemented**

Key issues: aid volume, channels and allocations

Recommendations 2010	Progress on implementation
As part of the 2012 budget proposal, i) set new realistic annual ODA volume targets that form a credible pathway for achieving the 0.7% ODA/GNI target by 2015; ii) work to build cross party support for achieving the new targets and growth path and publicise them widely; iii) replace debt relief with other types of development co-operation as the stock of debt becomes exhausted.	**Partially implemented**
Further concentrate its bilateral ODA on partner countries, particularly those in sub-Saharan Africa and countries affected by conflict and fragility.	**Partially implemented**

Key issues: organisation and management

Recommendations 2010	Progress on implementation
Ensure the merger of the three technical co-operation agencies is implemented on schedule and is seen as a first step in a holistic reform of Germany's development co-operation system.	**Implemented**
Implement the planned wider reforms of Germany's development co-operation system - the main aim should be to strengthen significantly BMZ's capacity to oversee the development and implementation of its own policies and to lead development co-operation policy effectively across the German government.	**Implemented**
Decentralise operations, as recommended in the last peer review, including developing a new understanding between BMZ and the Federal Foreign Office on their relationships in the field and strengthening and developing the role of focal area co-ordinators in partner countries.	**Partially implemented**

Key issues: delivery and partnerships

Recommendations 2010	Progress on implementation
Build on the progress made in implementing the aid effectiveness Plan of Operations by making greater use of partner country systems and adapting aid instruments to partner country-led programme-based approaches.	**Partially implemented**
Untie more technical co-operation, tailor it better to recipient countries' needs and align it more to country systems.	**Partially implemented**
Develop a strategy for how all of Germany's aid instruments (beyond technical co-operation) and agencies can develop capacity in partner countries, and how Germany will contribute to state building processes in fragile contexts.	**Implemented**
Develop a strategic framework for engagement with NGOs which clarifies its rationale for channelling funds through these organisations, defines its relationship with them, strengthens partnerships and ensures a focus on development results.	**Partially implemented**

Key issues: results management and accountability

Recommendations 2010	Progress on implementation
Ensure that i) adequate resources are allocated for improving evaluation and results reporting, including for the planned independent evaluation agency or institute; and ii) BMZ's country programming and resources are better linked to development results and aligned with effective partner country performance assessment frameworks.	**Partially implemented**

Key issues: humanitarian assistance

Recommendations 2010	Progress on implementation
Design an overarching humanitarian policy built on the comparative advantage of Germany's different instruments; strengthening linkages between relief and development programming; and continuing to increase humanitarian funding.	**Partially implemented**
Strengthen co-ordination of policy setting and strategic orientation issues and clarifying the division of labour between BMZ and the Federal Foreign Office; allowing partners to seek funding under a uniform proposal and reporting system; and strengthening thematic linkages between German humanitarian actors in government and civil society.	**Partially implemented**

Figure A.1 Germany's implementation of 2010 peer review recommendations

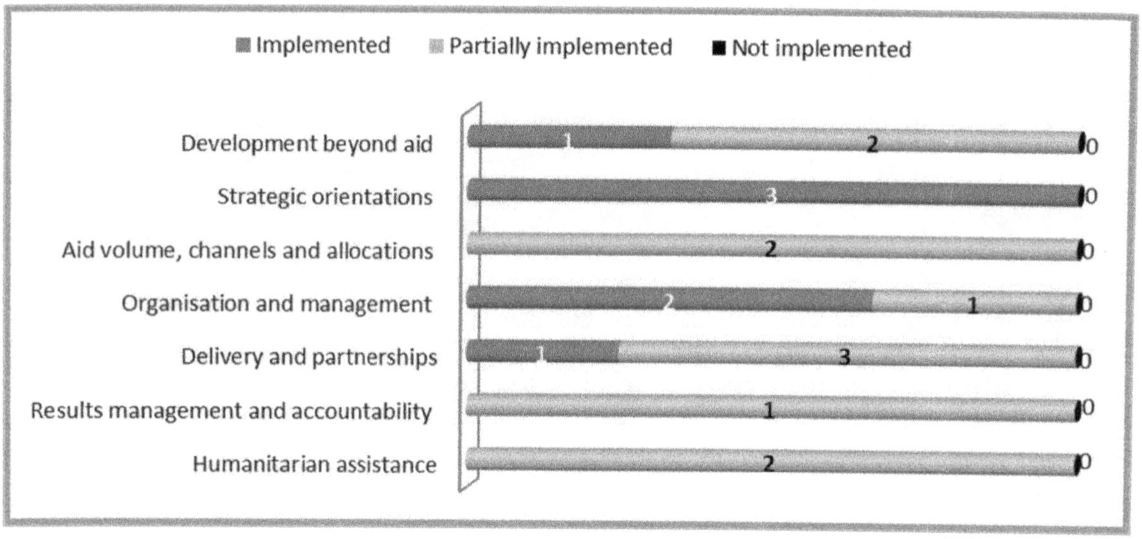

Annex B: OECD/DAC standard suite of tables

Table B.1 Total financial flows

USD million at current prices and exchange rates

							Net disbursements
Germany	**1999-2003**	**2004-2008**	**2009**	**2010**	**2011**	**2012**	**2013**
Total official flows	**5 298**	**10 322**	**12 266**	**12 578**	**13 683**	**12 094**	**13 862**
Official development assistance	**5 529**	**10 865**	**12 079**	**12 985**	**14 093**	**12 939**	**14 228**
Bilateral	3 241	7 063	7 097	8 036	8 736	8 584	9 451
Multilateral	2 288	3 801	4 983	4 950	5 357	4 355	4 777
Other official flows	**- 230**	**- 542**	**187**	**- 408**	**- 410**	**- 846**	**- 366**
Bilateral	- 203	- 542	187	- 408	- 410	- 846	- 366
Multilateral	- 27	-	-	-	-	-	-
Net Private Grants	**896**	**1 383**	**1 369**	**1 464**	**1 598**	**1 399**	**1 416**
Private flows at market terms	**4 029**	**17 173**	**15 495**	**27 595**	**40 921**	**21 224**	**35 942**
Bilateral: *of which*	4 730	17 109	14 325	27 931	41 308	21 395	35 830
Direct investment	2 843	11 053	12 941	21 991	29 875	15 763	18 300
Export credits	746	1 656	1 341	4 183	10 544	7 027	5 702
Multilateral	- 701	64	1 170	- 336	- 387	- 171	111
Total flows	**10 223**	**28 878**	**29 130**	**41 637**	**56 202**	**34 717**	**51 219**
for reference:							
ODA (at constant 2012 USD million)	*8 016*	*11 299*	*11 571*	*12 944*	*13 219*	*12 939*	*13 488*
ODA (as a % of GNI)	*0.27*	*0.35*	*0.35*	*0.39*	*0.39*	*0.37*	*0.38*
Total flows (as a % of GNI) (a)	*0.50*	*0.93*	*0.86*	*1.24*	*1.54*	*1.00*	*1.37*
ODA to and channelled through NGOs							
- In USD million	405	725	820	944	955	1 011	1 114
- In percentage of total net ODA	7	7	7	7	7	8	8
- DAC countries' average % of total net ODA	*8*	*8*	*7*	*8*	*9*	*13*	*13*

a. To countries eligible for ODA.

ODA net disbursements
At constant 2012 prices and exchange rates and as a share of GNI

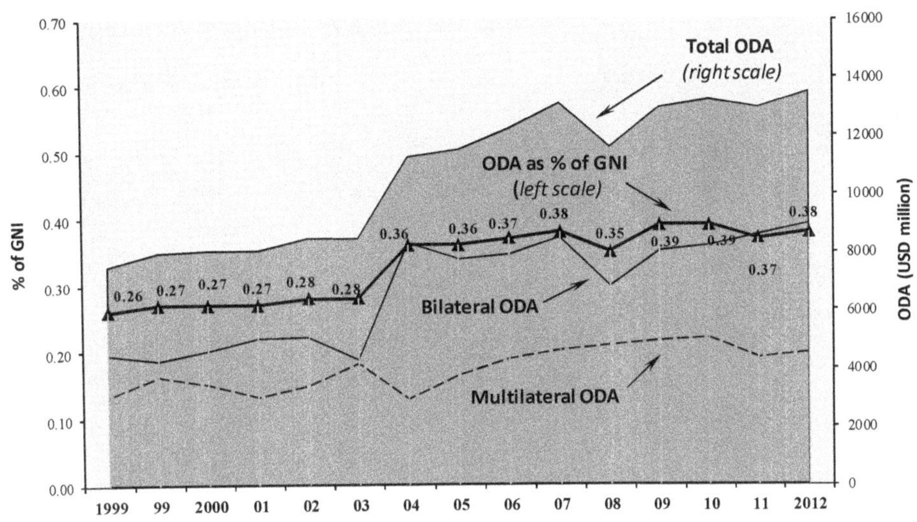

Table B.2 ODA by main categories

Disbursements

Germany	Constant 2012 USD million					Per cent share of gross disbursements					Total DAC 2013%
	2009	2010	2011	2012	2013	2009	2010	2011	2012	2013	
Gross Bilateral ODA	**8 008**	**9 407**	**9 605**	**10 214**	**10 848**	**63**	**66**	**66**	**70**	**71**	73
Budget support	-	128	414	66	37	-	1	3	0	0	4
of which: General budget support	130	97	142	58	35	1	1	1	0	0	2
Core contributions & pooled prog.& funds	-	1 265	633	674	442	-	9	4	5	3	13
of which: Core support to national NGOs	-	-	-	-	-	-	-	-	-	-	1
Core support to international NGOs	-	-	-	-	-	-	-	-	-	-	1
Core support to PPPs	-	13	154	6	56	-	0	1	0	0	0
Project-type interventions	-	5 386	5 818	6 329	7 186	-	38	40	43	47	39
of which: Investment projects	2 664	2 642	2 933	2 802	3 600	21	18	20	19	23	12
Experts and other technical assistance	-	834	741	610	896	-	6	5	4	6	4
Scholarships and student costs in donor countries	-	1 056	1 025	1 033	965	-	7	7	7	6	2
of which: Imputed student costs	884	884	867	887	844	7	6	6	6	5	1
Debt relief grants	144	164	425	849	572	1	1	3	6	4	4
Administrative costs	275	384	406	492	523	2	3	3	3	3	4
Other in-donor expenditures	92	138	142	160	219	1	1	1	1	1	3
of which: refugees in donor countries	67	81	81	76	132						
Gross Multilateral ODA	**4 773**	**4 934**	**5 025**	**4 355**	**4 529**	**37**	**34**	**34**	**30**	**29**	**27**
UN agencies	343	370	346	337	386	3	3	2	2	3	4
EU institutions	2 770	2 917	2 537	2 430	2 484	22	20	17	17	16	8
World Bank group	986	760	1 341	789	834	8	5	9	5	5	6
Regional development banks	266	298	291	314	315	2	2	2	2	2	3
Other multilateral	408	589	509	485	510	3	4	3	3	3	5
Total gross ODA	**12 781**	**14 341**	**14 629**	**14 570**	**15 377**	**100**	**100**	**100**	**100**	**100**	**100**
Repayments and debt cancellation	**-1 210**	**-1 397**	**-1 410**	**-1 630**	**-1 889**						
Total net ODA	**11 571**	**12 944**	**13 219**	**12 939**	**13 488**						
For reference:											
Free standing technical co-operation	*4 326*	*4 461*	*4 437*	*4 997*	*4 840*						
Net debt relief	*145*	*216*	*426*	*849*	*580*						

Contributions to UN Agencies (2012-13 Average)

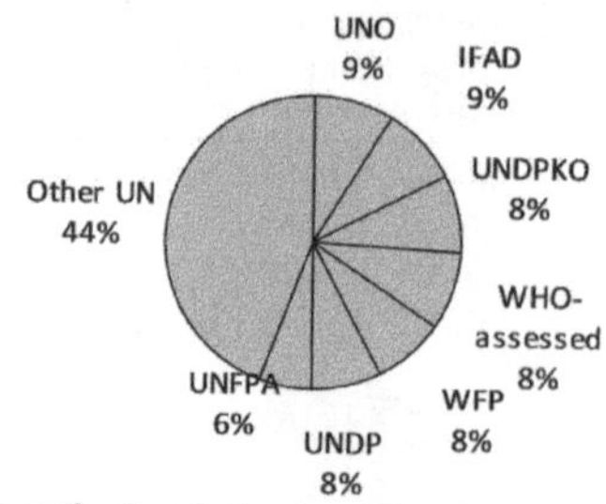

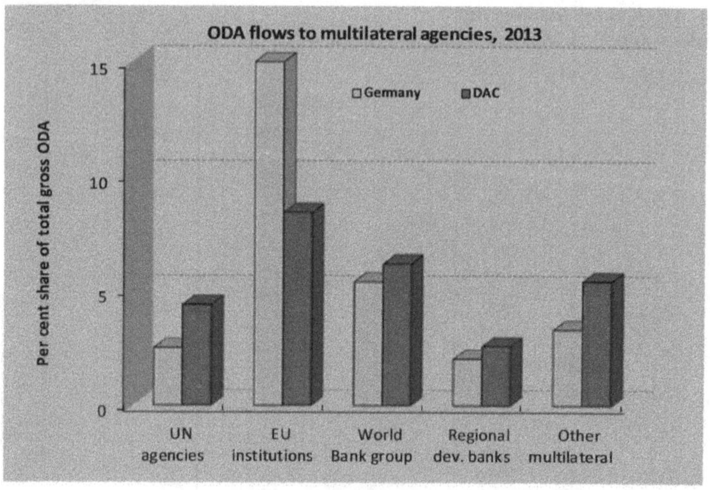

Contributions to Regional Development Banks (2012-13 Average)

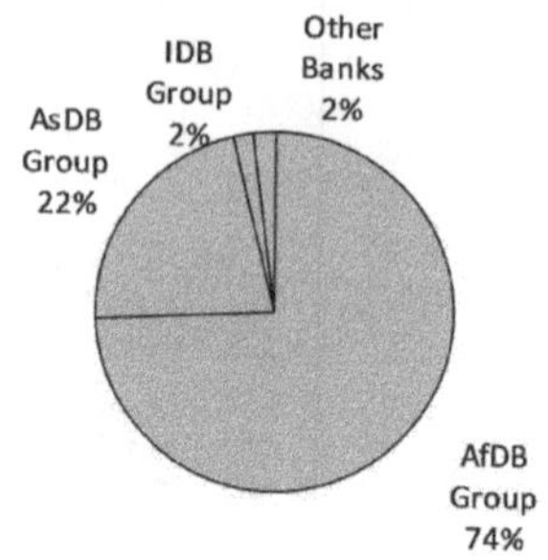

Table B.3 Bilateral ODA allocable by region and income group

Gross disbursements

Germany	Constant 2012 USD million					Per cent share					Total DAC
	2009	2010	2011	2012	2013	2009	2010	2011	2012	2013	2013%
Africa	2 201	2 195	2 673	3 217	2 913	32	30	33	38	32	**40**
Sub-Saharan Africa	1 559	1 627	1 977	2 529	1 981	23	22	24	30	22	**34**
North Africa	436	368	467	373	568	6	5	6	4	6	**4**
Asia	2 445	2 949	3 136	3 120	3 085	36	40	39	37	34	**37**
South and Central Asia	1 314	1 723	1 783	1 720	1 845	19	23	22	20	21	**24**
Far East	979	1 033	1 205	1 205	1 071	14	14	15	14	12	**12**
America	991	1 066	1 232	1 007	1 435	15	15	15	12	16	**9**
North and Central America	195	245	338	311	362	3	3	4	4	4	**4**
South America	528	652	726	562	643	8	9	9	7	7	**4**
Middle East	454	460	455	570	807	7	6	6	7	9	**9**
Oceania	6	5	10	13	14	0	0	0	0	0	**2**
Europe	703	673	600	576	736	10	9	7	7	8	**3**
Total bilateral allocable by region	**6 800**	**7 348**	**8 105**	**8 504**	**8 990**	**100**	**100**	**100**	**100**	**100**	**100**
Least developed	1 585	1 770	1 864	2 351	1 712	27	28	27	33	24	**45**
Other low-income	175	184	284	485	196	3	3	4	7	3	**4**
Lower middle-income	2 066	2 348	2 521	2 224	3 074	36	38	36	31	42	**35**
Upper middle-income	1 926	1 925	2 280	2 132	2 288	33	31	33	30	31	**16**
More advanced developing countries	29	28	-	-	-	1	0	-	-	-	**-**
Total bilateral allocable by income	**5 780**	**6 255**	**6 948**	**7 192**	**7 270**	**100**	**100**	**100**	**100**	**100**	**100**
For reference:											
Total bilateral	8 008	9 407	9 605	10 214	10 848	*100*	*100*	*100*	*100*	*100*	***100***
of which: Unallocated by region	*1 209*	*2 059*	*1 500*	*1 711*	*1 858*	*15*	*22*	*16*	*17*	*17*	***25***
of which: Unallocated by income	*2 228*	*3 151*	*2 656*	*3 022*	*3 579*	*28*	*34*	*28*	*30*	*33*	***31***

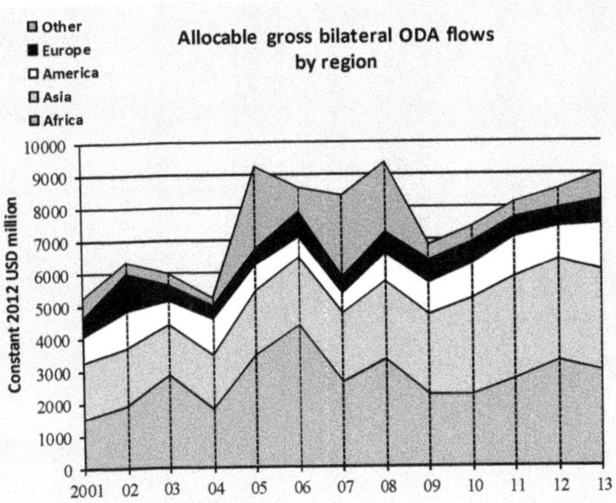

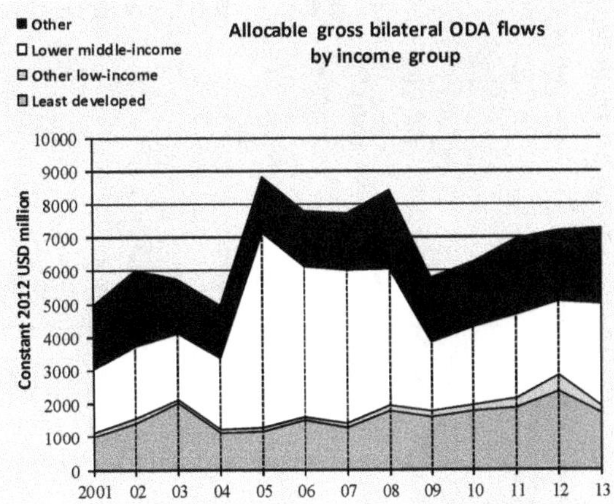

1. Each region includes regional amounts which cannot be allocated by sub-region. The sum of the sub-regional amounts may therefore fall short of the regional total.

Table B.4 Main recipients of bilateral ODA

Gross disbursements

Germany	2002-06 average Current USD million	Constant 2012 USD mln	Per cent share	Memo: DAC countries' average %
Nigeria	625	696	10	
Iraq	494	553	8	
China (People's Republic of)	392	468	6	
Cameroon	220	262	3	
Serbia	205	274	3	
Top 5 recipients	**1 936**	**2 253**	**30**	**50**
India	170	207	3	
Indonesia	170	200	3	
Democratic Republic of the Congo	147	180	2	
Zambia	144	169	2	
Nicaragua	139	163	2	
Top 10 recipients	**2 707**	**3 173**	**41**	**68**
Egypt	134	160	2	
Bolivia	121	166	2	
Turkey	111	136	2	
Ghana	107	124	2	
Afghanistan	100	124	2	
Top 15 recipients	**3 281**	**3 883**	**50**	**76**
Morocco	91	107	1	
Mozambique	83	112	1	
Brazil	80	96	1	
Viet Nam	79	93	1	
Peru	74	88	1	
Top 20 recipients	**3 689**	**4 378**	**56**	**80**
Total (147 recipients)	5 580	6 649	85	
Unallocated	981	1 164	15	5
Total bilateral gross	**6 561**	**7 813**	**100**	**100**

	2007-11 average Current USD million	Constant 2012 USD mln	Per cent share	Memo: DAC countries' average %
Iraq	811	784	8	
China (People's Republic of)	578	556	6	
India	461	444	5	
Afghanistan	372	358	4	
Cameroon	323	313	3	
Top 5 recipients	**2 545**	**2 454**	**26**	**37**
Indonesia	210	202	2	
Egypt	194	187	2	
Brazil	185	178	2	
Morocco	144	139	1	
Turkey	141	135	1	
Top 10 recipients	**3 418**	**3 296**	**35**	**51**
Liberia	131	124	1	
Peru	128	121	1	
Pakistan	119	114	1	
Serbia	117	113	1	
Viet Nam	114	109	1	
Top 15 recipients	**4 026**	**3 877**	**42**	**55**
South Africa	113	109	1	
Kenya	102	98	1	
West Bank and Gaza Strip	97	93	1	
Ethiopia	94	91	1	
Tanzania	94	90	1	
Top 20 recipients	**4 526**	**4 358**	**47**	**58**
Total (149 recipients)	7 293	7 021	75	
Unallocated	2 392	2 307	25	24
Total bilateral gross	**9 685**	**9 328**	**100**	**100**

	2012-13 average Current USD million	Constant 2012 USD mln	Per cent share	Memo: DAC countries average %
China (People's Republic of)	682	666	6	
India	610	590	6	
Afghanistan	532	518	5	
Democratic Republic of the Congo	344	342	3	
Côte d'Ivoire	262	248	2	
Top 5 recipients	**2 430**	**2 363**	**22**	**36**
Kenya	235	232	2	
Turkey	219	211	2	
Egypt	216	208	2	
Syrian Arab Republic	209	201	2	
Brazil	208	201	2	
Top 10 recipients	**3 517**	**3 417**	**32**	**50**
Pakistan	149	145	1	
Mexico	139	135	1	
Viet Nam	130	126	1	
West Bank and Gaza Strip	127	124	1	
Indonesia	121	118	1	
Top 15 recipients	**4 184**	**4 065**	**39**	**57**
Peru	116	113	1	
Morocco	104	100	1	
Ethiopia	101	99	1	
Yemen	98	95	1	
Bangladesh	97	94	1	
Top 20 recipients	**4 699**	**4 566**	**43**	**61**
Total (138 recipients)	7 430	7 231	69	
Unallocated	3 398	3 300	31	28
Total bilateral gross	**10 829**	**10 531**	**100**	**100**

Table B.5 Bilateral ODA by major purposes

at constant prices and exchange rates

Commitments - Two-year average

Germany	2002-2006 average		2007-11 average		2012-13 average		2012-13
	2012 USD million	Per cent	2012 USD million	Per cent	2012 USD million	Per cent	Total DAC per cent
Social infrastructure & services	**2 663**	**32**	**4 286**	**40**	**5 439**	**43**	**39**
Education	1094	13	1 666	16	1 891	15	8
of which: basic education	116	1	168	2	183	1	2
Health	191	2	260	2	481	4	6
of which: basic health	107	1	152	1	339	3	4
Population & reproductive health	131	2	157	1	186	1	7
Water supply & sanitation	454	6	790	7	1 197	9	5
Government & civil society	520	6	1 249	12	1 498	12	12
of which: Conflict, peace & security	50	1	305	3	333	3	2
Other social infrastructure & services	272	3	166	2	187	1	2
Economic infrastructure & services	**1148**	**14**	**2 441**	**23**	**3 370**	**27**	**18**
Transport & storage	234	3	206	2	193	2	8
Communications	17	0	13	0	23	0	0
Energy	473	6	1 262	12	1 666	13	6
Banking & financial services	296	4	778	7	1 255	10	2
Business & other services	128	2	182	2	233	2	1
Production sectors	**355**	**4**	**529**	**5**	**674**	**5**	**7**
Agriculture, forestry & fishing	258	3	352	3	450	4	5
Industry, mining & construction	75	1	129	1	185	1	1
Trade & tourism	21	0	48	0	38	0	1
Multisector	**918**	**11**	**1 121**	**11**	**1 646**	**13**	**9**
Commodity and programme aid	**81**	**1**	**169**	**2**	**134**	**1**	**4**
Action relating to debt	**2 447**	**30**	**1 318**	**12**	**334**	**3**	**3**
Humantarian aid	**293**	**4**	**347**	**3**	**471**	**4**	**9**
Administrative costs of donors	**285**	**3**	**352**	**3**	**535**	**4**	**6**
Refugees in donor countries	**25**	**0**	**62**	**1**	**104**	**1**	**4**
Total bilateral allocable	8 214	100	10 627	100	12 706	100	100
For reference:							
Total bilateral	*8 322*	*69*	*10 673*	*65*	*12 802*	*72*	*74*
of which: Unallocated	*108*	*1*	*46*	*0*	*96*	*1*	*1*
Total multilateral	*3 780*	*31*	*5 688*	*35*	*4 971*	*28*	*26*
Total ODA	***12 102***	***100***	***16 361***	***100***	***17 773***	***100***	***100***

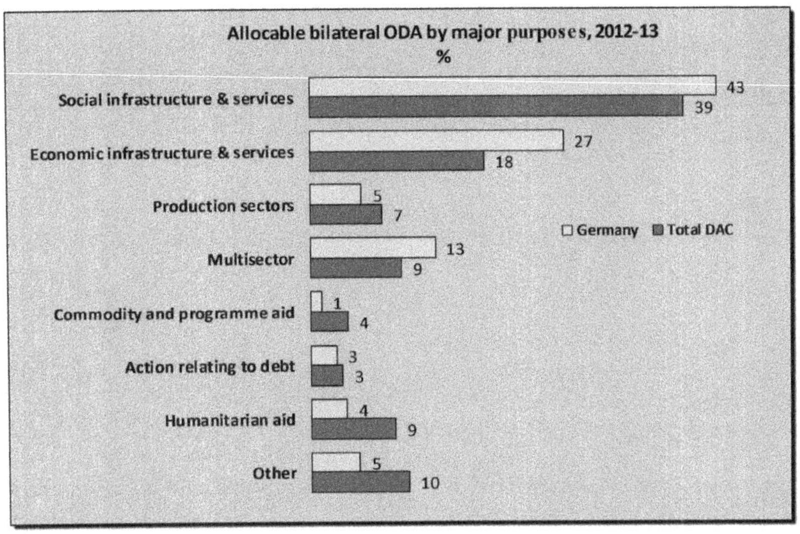

Table B.6 Comparative aid performance

Net disbursements

	Official development assistance			Grant element of ODA (commitments)	Share of multilateral aid				ODA to LDCs Bilateral and through multilateral agencies	
	2013		2007-08 to 2012-13 Average annual % change in real terms	2013	2013				2013	
					% of ODA		% of GNI			
	USD million	% of GNI		% (a)	(b)	(c)	(b)	(c)	% of ODA	% of GNI
Australia	4 846	0.33	6.0	99.9	14.0		0.05		27.6	0.09
Austria	1 171	0.27	-8.6	100.0	53.6	28.1	0.15	0.08	29.2	0.08
Belgium	2 300	0.45	1.0	99.8	43.2	21.6	0.20	0.10	35.4	0.16
Canada	4 947	0.27	0.9	100.0	29.0		0.08		37.4	0.10
Czech Republic	211	0.11	0.5	100.0	73.0	16.9	0.08	0.02	24.8	0.03
Denmark	2 927	0.85	0.2	100.0	26.8	17.9	0.23	0.15	31.6	0.27
Finland	1 435	0.54	4.6	100.0	42.7	28.9	0.23	0.15	35.5	0.19
France	11 342	0.41	2.6	84.4	40.0	20.0	0.16	0.08	30.4	0.12
Germany	14 228	0.38	0.9	86.9	33.6	15.2	0.13	0.06	23.7	0.09
Greece	239	0.10	-13.4	100.0	81.8	6.5	0.08	0.01	18.7	0.02
Iceland	35	0.25	-5.2	100.0	15.8		0.04		46.0	0.12
Ireland	846	0.46	-5.7	100.0	35.5	20.0	0.16	0.09	50.4	0.23
Italy	3 407	0.17	-7.0	99.8	75.0	27.5	0.12	0.05	28.1	0.05
Japan	11 582	0.23	2.1	89.1	25.6		0.06		60.5	0.14
Korea	1 755	0.13	16.7	95.1	25.4		0.03		40.6	0.05
Luxembourg	429	1.00	-0.9	100.0	30.4	21.5	0.30	0.22	37.9	0.38
Netherlands	5 435	0.67	-3.2	100.0	32.9	21.0	0.22	0.14	25.1	0.17
New Zealand	457	0.26	1.6	100.0	23.3		0.06		32.4	0.09
Norway	5 581	1.07	2.9	100.0	22.7		0.24		27.6	0.30
Poland	472	0.10	5.7	..	74.4	6.1	0.07	0.01	26.5	0.03
Portugal	488	0.23	0.6	87.7	38.0	5.8	0.09	0.01	29.3	0.07
Slovak Republic	86	0.09	0.1	100.0	81.2	12.1	0.08	0.01	24.4	0.02
Slovenia	62	0.13	0.1	100.0	66.5	12.7	0.09	0.02	17.5	0.02
Spain	2 375	0.17	-17.2	100.0	60.2	16.7	0.10	0.03	18.9	0.03
Sweden	5 827	1.01	2.3	100.0	32.8	26.4	0.33	0.27	31.0	0.31
Switzerland	3 197	0.47	6.1	100.0	21.6		0.10		25.9	0.12
United Kingdom	17 920	0.71	9.8	100.0	41.2	30.5	0.29	0.22	34.6	0.24
United States	30 879	0.18	3.5	100.0	14.6		0.03		33.1	0.06
Total DAC	**134 481**	**0.30**	**2.0**	**95.1**	**30.4**		**0.09**		**33.3**	**0.10**
Memo: Average country effoı		0.39								

Notes:

a. Excluding debt reorganisation.

b. Including EU institutions.

c. Excluding EU institutions.

.. Data not available.

Figure B.1 Net ODA from DAC countries in 2013

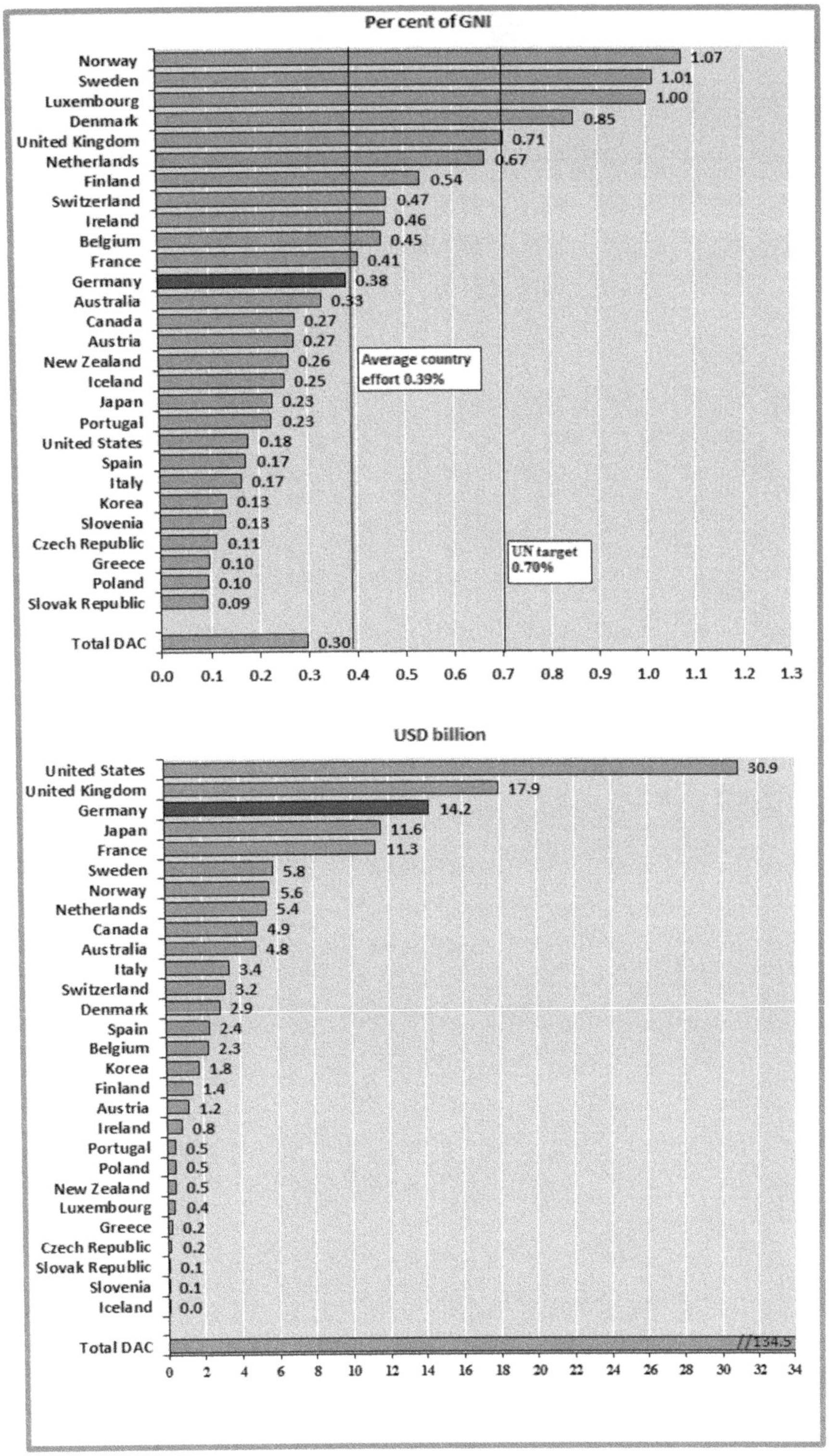

Annex C: Visits to Mozambique and Kenya

As part of the peer review of Germany, a team of examiners and the OECD secretariat visited Kenya and Mozambique in February and March 2015. In both countries the team met with the Ambassador of Germany and heads of sections of the German embassy; the German development co-operation team, including the GIZ and KfW country directors, senior programme managers and locally recruited staff; partner government officials in charge of development co-operation and in line ministries; parliamentarians; bilateral and multilateral partners; and German and local civil society organisations.

Towards a comprehensive German development effort

Germany's vision of sustainable development is reflected in Kenya and Mozambique

Mozambique is a rapidly growing country of an estimated 25 million people that has experienced significant economic recovery since its devastating 16-year civil war ended in 1992. In recent years Mozambique's gross domestic product has grown at an average annual rate of 7.5%. The recent discoveries of vast gas reserves and other minerals give Mozambique the opportunity for major economic growth, yet it remains a poor country, ranking 178 out of 187 on the 2014 Human Development Index. It also has to deal regularly with natural disasters, mainly floods, droughts and cyclones. Mozambique's challenge will be to translate its natural wealth into equitable and inclusive growth.

Kenya achieved lower middle-income status in 2012, and had an economic growth rate of 4.7% in 2013. The population is estimated at 44.4 million and poverty has declined from 47% in 2005 to 34-42% recently. However, Kenya is in the low human development category, ranking 147 out of 187 on the 2014 Human Development Index. Its economy is based on only a small number of exports: mainly tea, coffee and cut flowers. The country is currently facing challenges related to inequality, governance, low investment and low firm productivity. In the Northern region, the Somalia-based Al Shabaab and local militias pose a serious security problem.

Mozambique and Kenya are not dependent on international assistance to the same extent. The amount of external aid represents, on average, 15% of Mozambique's gross national income, and 7% of Kenya's.

Germany's engagement in Mozambique and Kenya builds on long-term relationships spanning several decades and focuses now on promoting broader sustainable development objectives, consistent with Germany's holistic vision for the 2030 Agenda. In both countries, in addition to supporting human development, Germany targets good financial governance and increasing domestic resource mobilisation, as well as promoting private investment by engaging with local, German and international companies. As an example of good practice, BMZ helped to set-up a German Chamber of Commerce and Industry office in Maputo to increase co-ordination between foreign trade promotion and development policy, engage private sector companies in development and leverage socially responsible business. In Kenya, Germany's support in the energy sector is targeting efficient use of energy and renewable energy (wind power, geothermal). Looking ahead, Germany plans to support Kenya's economic potential and foster greater regional integration, with the view to moving beyond development co-operation in the long term.

Mechanisms exist to ensure consistent approaches in Kenya and Mozambique

In Kenya, Germany has a broad presence in different areas and involves several German ministries, including a representative from the Ministry of Environment posted to the embassy. In addition to internal co-ordination mechanisms, the embassy engages in regular dialogue with other German actors (including the four political foundations represented in Kenya). Guided by the federal government's policy guidelines for Africa, the embassy has comprehensive joined-up approaches in a number of areas, particularly as regards peace and conflict. The government-to-government consultation and negotiation process to define the development co-operation programme includes all relevant German ministries.

The situation is different in Mozambique, where development co-operation up to now has been the main area of Germany's involvement. The embassy only houses staff from the Federal Foreign Office and staff seconded from BMZ. While economic relationships are increasing, involvement by other ministries remains limited, lessening the need for co-ordination.

The German embassies in Mozambique and Kenya, as is the case for all German embassies, report regularly to the Federal Foreign Office on political analysis and development issues. This provides an opportunity to identify areas where there are competing interests among various German policies and to look for consistency. As an example, the economic and development co-operation sections of the German Embassy prepared a joint report on Kenya' economic partnership agreement with the European Union to ensure their perspectives were mutually reinforcing.

Germany is creative in using ODA to catalyse other resources

In both countries, Germany has a comprehensive approach to using ODA as a catalyst, drawing on a range of tools and actors. In Mozambique, Germany:

- encourages private sector engagement by helping to build an enabling environment for private investment, crowding in private capital via public-private partnerships and a range of services provided to economic players in Germany, and supporting the improvement of trade capacity and conditions;
- helps mobilise domestic resources, providing support to strengthen the Mozambican tax authority, improve fiscal transparency and management, generate local revenue for municipalities and improve public financial management within local governments;
- mobilises additional German and international resources, engaging with Brazil in triangular co-operation projects, providing additional funding for climate change, and extending KfW promotional loans to boost the Mozambican economy.

In Kenya, where Germany has a growing business presence, the same multi-layered approach applies, although with a stronger focus on fighting corruption, a key impediment to economic investment in Kenya. GIZ promotes partnerships with the private sector (46 development partnerships since 1999), KfW mobilises additional funding through interest-subsidised and promotional loans and develops results-based mechanisms to attract private sector investments, and DEG actively promotes responsible business growth. DEG supports 24 companies with a portfolio of EUR 179 million invested, among others, in the finance sector (43%), energy (24%) and mining (16%). Meanwhile Germany has invested EUR 15.2 million in development partnerships with the private sector.

Germany's policies, strategies and aid allocations

Kenya and Mozambique are long-term partners

Germany has engaged in development co-operation for more than 50 years with Kenya, and for some 30 years with Mozambique. Germany is one of the top donors in Kenya, committing EUR 390 million between 2010 and 2013 and EUR 294 million from 2014 to 2017. Spending an average of EUR 75 million every year, the Kenya programme is larger than in Mozambique, where Germany provides about EUR 60 million every year, committing EUR 117 million in 2012-13 and EUR 128 million over 2014-15.

Germany focuses on poverty reduction and institutional development

Germany's relationship with Kenya and Mozambique is characterised by high-quality policy dialogue and its valued contribution to institution building. In both Mozambique and Kenya, Germany is seen as a reliable and predictable donor, responsive to evolving needs within its focus sectors. Germany's objective in both countries is clearly to reduce poverty, and to do so in line with their own national priorities.

In Mozambique, Germany's programme is strategically concentrated in three key sectors (education, decentralisation, and sustainable economic development) and three provinces (Inhambane, Manica and Sofala). The long-term engagement in these sectors and geographic areas has allowed Germany to develop deep knowledge of the context and to have greater impact.

In Kenya, Germany is also focusing on three sectors (agriculture and rural development, water and sanitation, and health). In response to Kenyan government's requests, Germany has also maintained a targeted programme in education, governance and energy. Germany uses a wide variety of instruments with a clear rationale, including for providing grants and concessional loans in a middle-income country. In the water sector, for example, Germany provides grants to the Water Services Trust Fund, an institution which has been established to finance pro-poor infrastructure in urban informal settlements, while financing water and sanitation facilitation in Nairobi is done through a promotional loan.

In 2014 the bilateral programme in Kenya (as well as German NGOs) received funding from the new special initiatives on refugees (Fighting the Root Causes of Displacement, Reintegrating Refugees) and food security (One World, No Hunger). These came on top of the regular programme established through government-to-government negotiations. The quick disbursements required under these initiatives can prove challenging for the organisations involved, since their separate planning and reporting requirements make it difficult to integrate funding into existing programmes and risk undermining the coherence of development programmes.

The response to the 2011 drought emergency demonstrates Germany's capacity to create holistic, phased responses, bringing together the various humanitarian instruments. Germany could build on this and develop more systematic links between funding tools, programmes and German funded partners, over a longer-term timeframe, to help build resilience to Kenya's protracted crisis situations.

In both countries, Germany takes a context-specific approach to cross-cutting issues. In Kenya, it focuses now on anti-corruption and climate change while continuing to promote gender equality. In Mozambique, cross-cutting issues are dealt with comprehensively in a sector such as education. However, it is unclear the extent to which these cross-cutting issues are dealt with rigorously in all sectors, despite the fact that appropriate tools exist, such as a gender-HIV/AIDs focal point in GIZ. In both countries, there is limited evidence showing how policy dialogue addresses cross-cutting issues systematically.

Organisation and management

Institutional reforms are having positive results

The institutional reforms of Germany's development co-operation are having good results in bilateral country programmes. The doubling of BMZ staff seconded to the embassy, from one to two, allows the embassy to lead on policy dialogue, drawing on the expertise of the implementing agencies. Implementing agencies welcome such a leading role for the embassy as they benefit from a higher level of access to government. Strengthened BMZ country presence can also better inform decision making within the ministry. The "heads of co-operation" positions are strategic and require high-calibre staff. This should be recognised in staff career pathways and accompanied by a commensurate access to learning and exchange opportunities.

In both Kenya and Mozambique, Germany's development co-operation speaks with one voice, reinforcing the role of Germany as a key partner. Steered by a cohesive country team under the leadership of heads of co-operation in embassies, the agencies complement one another and look for synergies in designing joint programmes at the sector level. While the embassy leads on policy dialogue, implementing agencies contribute to this dialogue depending on the context and resources available in country. Staff in both the embassy and the implementing agencies are dealing pragmatically with the division of labour, recognising that flexibility and good information sharing are essential for the country team to work effectively. The colocation of GIZ and KfW within the "German House" facilitates the smooth exchange of information.

The merger of the three technical agencies into GIZ has been achieved by integrating their various instruments into the sector management lines. The reduced fragmentation has meant greater efficiency and strategic coherence, improving the relevance of each instrument. In both countries, development workers are well integrated within GIZ programmes, reducing transaction costs for the German stakeholders and their partners. GIZ in Mozambique indicated that, in the absence of quota, they might have come up with a smaller number of development workers, on the basis of actual programme needs.

Decision making remains centralised

Germany's decision making remains centralised, which lengthens the programming process and creates distance from local partners. The complex information feedback loop between BMZ, the Federal Foreign Office and the implementing agencies, in headquarters and the field, creates additional challenges. This can result in missed opportunities and a lack of flexibility, undermining the quality of partnerships and Germany's ability to build consensus. Now that the reform has increased capacity in the embassy, decentralising more authority to this level seems the logical next step.

While GIZ is guided by strong leadership in country offices, responsibility for managing projects in KfW remains largely at headquarters. In the context of Kenya's complex programme, Mozambique's weak capacities, and fiduciary risks in general, increased delegation of authority backed up by additional field presence and greater empowerment of local managers could enable programme implementation to be more responsive to the local context.

Teams are appreciated and benefit from a good working environment

In Kenya and Mozambique, Germany benefits from a strong and highly appreciated team of international and national staff. In total, there are about 260 staff working for the German development co-operation in Mozambique and 220 in Kenya, with 60 and 55 expatriate staff respectively (Table C.1). While GIZ offices are well staffed, reflecting the decentralised way in which German technical co-operation is delivered, KfW's staffing numbers in country are limited - particularly in Mozambique (Table C.1). KfW has more staff in Kenya, which facilitates interaction with partners.

With a total of three development co-operation staff to cover two countries (Kenya and Somalia), the German Embassy in Kenya seems short of staff, especially given the ambitious programme in Kenya and the complex situation in Somalia.

Table C.1 German development co-operation in Mozambique and Kenya – Staffing levels in 2015 (full-time equivalent)

Staff numbers	Mozambique		Kenya	
	International	Locally recruited	International	Locally recruited
Embassy	3.3	0.5	2.5	0.5
GIZ	55*	200	50*	150
KfW/DEG	1.5	5	3 (+ 2 in DEG)	11

**This includes long-term expatriates, international contracts, development workers and integrated experts.*

Source: figures provided to the review team in Maputo and Nairobi.

GIZ and KfW have created a positive working and learning culture. As an illustration, a "Kenya connectivity group" was set up in Nairobi to encourage young Kenyan staff to share innovative ideas and advice based on their knowledge of the Kenyan context with the GIZ management team. This management team also comprises two locally-recruited staff. While GIZ offers a fulfilling career path to local staff, such opportunities are more limited in KfW and the embassy, with their organisational structure and smaller staff numbers. A range of stakeholders noted that BMZ's requirement for key documents to be in German inevitably imposes some limitations on opportunities for local staff advancement, and prevents full transparency and engagement with local partners on planning and reporting.

Partnerships

Government-to-government negotiations define programmes

Germany defines its country programmes during bilateral negotiations with partner country governments – every three years in Kenya and every two years in Mozambique. These negotiations involve high-level representatives from BMZ and the ministries of finance in the two respective countries. The partner governments, including line ministries in focus sectors, are widely consulted from an early stage in preparing the bilateral negotiations. They are also invited to identify specific project proposals. As a follow-up to bilateral negotiations, Germany signs a legally-binding agreement with partner country governments. Such an agreement enables GIZ and KfW to develop individual programme proposals and BMZ to commit resources over future years.

In both Kenya and Mozambique, however, Germany has yet to finalise country strategies. While in Mozambique, the embassy decided justifiably to postpone the process until after the 2014 election, the country strategy for Kenya has now reached its final stage of preparation, currently undergoing final review within BMZ. These country strategies, which are expected to cover two programming cycles, will reinforce the strategic approach needed for building capacity over the long term while bringing greater predictability.

Greater budget predictability and flexibility are needed

Currently, information on Germany's future development co-operation spending is limited to two to three years ahead (depending on the frequency of bilateral negotiations). The introduction of country strategies could increase predictability to up to six years ahead, on a rolling basis, but only if information on forward-looking expenditure is included.

Although GIZ and KfW are increasingly developing joint proposals in focus sectors to maximise synergies between their instruments, the fixed allocation of funding between financial and technical co-operation can prevent German development co-operation from responding fully to priorities of partner countries. In addition, several stakeholders noted how the lack of flexibility in reallocating funds across budget lines and years within individual programmes is a constraint in adapting to evolving situations and needs.

While Germany has been seen as a reliable and predictable partner, the introduction of variable tranches linked to performance in the education sector may undermine Mozambique's ability to plan and execute its programmes. In addition to a fixed annual contribution of about EUR 15 million to the education basked fund, Germany introduced a performance-based tranche whose release is linked to progress in school construction, using the Ministry of Education's planning and review process to make decisions and spelling out the milestones to be achieved for releasing additional funds. Although the condition is only for the additional tranche to encourage the government to build more classrooms, it is not easy for the government to plan for additional funding which may not come through.

Use of country systems varies across sectors and modalities

In Kenya, KfW uses Kenyan government procurement, reporting and audit systems. As is the case for most other donors, fiduciary risks mean that German funds are not passed through Kenya's national treasury. Instead, Germany uses a "direct payment" modality, whereby KfW pays contractors on behalf of the Kenyan government. Additional safeguard measures include the use of an internationally recruited tender agent who assists the government for procuring goods and services.

Germany provided budget support in Mozambique until 2014. In the context of declining support for the instrument due to political reasons, the programme was ended following a decision by the German Parliament. The decision was announced during the 2014 bilateral negotiations. However, Germany was able to swiftly reallocate the resources previously channelled through budget support to ensure that the funding could be made available for Mozambique. Meanwhile German support to the education sector is aligned with the government of Mozambique's education sector plan and integrated into the annual programming and reporting process of the Ministry of Education. German support combines technical co-operation with financial co-operation, consisting of contributions to a multi-donor pooled funding mechanism.

Capacity development works at multiple levels

Germany's approach to capacity development combines work at the national and sub-national levels. Technical and financial co-operation are mutually supportive, helping to develop synergies among the different levels and piloting approaches that can be replicated. This is well illustrated by German support to Mozambique's education sector:

- At the macro level, technical co-operation involves advice to the Ministry of Education in implementing the sector plan and reforming technical and vocational education, while financial co-operation helps strengthen country systems through policy-based programme finance and dialogue.
- At the intermediate level, technical co-operation supports provincial and district authorities in managing the education sector, including schools and teacher training facilities.
- At the micro level, financial co-operation supports the Ministry of Education to fund and implement school-building programmes, while technical co-operation provides direct support to schools, particularly for technical and vocational training.

To strengthen their approach, GIZ and KfW may consider how project design and procurement practices can better engage local resources. In Mozambique, several partners raised concerns about not being sufficiently involved in selecting consultants. In Kenya, some partners also mentioned that the use of German procedures tended to slow down implementation. While Germany's technical co-operation is appreciated, there may be benefits in using the various instruments more flexibly and in maximising the role of partner structures in programme implementation.

Germany works closely with other partners through co-ordination mechanisms and delegated co-operation

In both Kenya and Mozambique, Germany engages actively with other development partners and leads on a number of key donor co-ordination and sector working groups, bringing in solid expertise that is widely appreciated. The embassy, with its strengthened BMZ presence, dedicates appropriate resources to these tasks, and can get additional resources when chairing a working group. In Mozambique, for example, the embassy plans to mobilise additional capacity locally to support the Head of Co-operation, now that Germany will take the lead in the education sector donor group in early 2016. In Kenya, the head of co-operation leads the Development Partners' Group, together with the African Development Bank, the main group for co-ordinating all development partners (Box C.1). In addition, the embassy's Head of Co-operation also draws on the sector expertise within the country team to engage meaningfully in policy dialogue while GIZ and KfW continue to engage in some technical working groups.

Other donors are increasingly relying on GIZ and KfW's implementation capacity in the form of delegated co-operation agreements. For instance, in Mozambique, GIZ is implementing an HIV/AIDS programme on behalf of the European Commission. In Kenya, it has developed an integrity and accountability programme, addressing corruption through the entire range of relevant reforms. Germany's comprehensive approach has encouraged Sweden to put funding into it and other donors might follow suit. KfW also works closely with other international financial institutions through co-financing arrangements, as is the case in Kenya for large infrastructure projects.

Germany is a strong supporter of EU joint programming globally and at country level. In Kenya, the German Embassy has been instrumental in driving the process forward, bringing personal commitment with political backing. In this country, EU member states see the joint strategy as a first step towards joint engagement, identifying opportunities for working together pragmatically so as to have greater impact collectively through collaboration. The situation is different in Mozambique, where discussions on EU joint programming are more preliminary. However, Germany plays a constructive broker role to overcome some of the challenges associated with the overall weak co-ordination mechanism at the political level (Box C.1), which affects the extent to which EU member states can progress on joint programming.

Box C.1 Policy dialogue and co-ordination mechanisms in Mozambique and Kenya

Mozambique's policy dialogue and co-ordination mechanisms around general budget support have long been considered a model of strong partnership which helped the country recover from 16 years of civil war. The robustness of policy dialogue within the "G19" - the initial group of 6 like-minded donors providing general budget as early as 2000 has expanded to include 22 members since 2008 – is based on a common memorandum of understanding, a mutual framework of commitments between the government and donors and a performance assessment framework. As a result, the G19 has become the main platform for policy dialogue and donor co-ordination, including a complex system of joint working groups and sub-groups, while the Development Partners Group — initially established for facilitating government-donor dialogue — appears to have been relegated to an information-sharing role. Meanwhile, the mandate of the G19 has evolved beyond general budget support, with donors not providing general budget support invited as associate members. At the same time, several bilateral donors decided to provide small amounts of general budget support to become a full member of the G19. This generated tensions between donors providing small financial contributions, interested mainly in participating in the policy dialogue, and other donors, who also need a platform for discussing aspects of a more technical nature. The decision of several donors to stop providing general budget support to Mozambique in recent years created some discomfort within the government, which considers that donors do not always apply conditionality transparently, undermining the spirit of a true partnership. This decision also means that the overall co-ordination mechanism needs to be reshaped, distinguishing between broader policy dialogue and engagement in general budget support. Such a change would also provide an opportunity to bring in emerging economies, who are increasingly active in the country, and make dialogue evolve to take into consideration different co-operation modalities, in light of new economic opportunities and a more diverse range of actors.

In Kenya, the high-level policy dialogue between the government and development partners takes place in the Development Partnership Forum, which brings together heads of government departments, diplomatic missions and development agencies. The government and development partners meet on a monthly basis in separate groups; the main donor co-ordination group is the Development Partners' Group, while the Aid Effectiveness Group, with its secretariat located in the National Treasury, ensures co-ordination between the government and development partners at working level. Several sector working groups also meet regularly around the priorities defined in *Vision 2030*, Kenya's long term development strategy, and the sectors defined by the medium term expenditure framework. Despite well-established structures, Kenya does not benefit from a strong framework for mutual accountability and has not made much progress in implementing Busan commitments. In addition, dialogue seems to have lost momentum since the adoption of the Kenya's Joint Assistance Strategy (2007-12), which played, at that time, an important role in strengthening government – donor relationships.

Engagement with NGOs could be more systematic

In both Kenya and Mozambique, Germany has good interaction with German and local NGOs and supports a wide range of organisations. Most support to local NGOs is channelled through German NGOs, which apply for project funding in headquarters. Some local NGOs benefit from small grants through the embassy. In some cases, German and local NGOs can be involved in German development co-operation programmes by being directly contracted by GIZ and KfW. In Kenya, some German NGOs have been able to access funding through the special initiatives and welcome the flexibility in the system -

though some stakeholders raised concerns about being used as implementers and facing difficulties in spending the money within a year. Given this diversity of funding sources, German NGOs would appreciate greater clarity on how to access funding, including more information on the website or through the creation of a single online platform.

While there are good synergies between German implementing agencies and NGOs at an operational level, there is scope for more mutual learning with and among NGOs. Although the German Embassy in Kenya organises regular meetings on specific issues, German NGOs indicated that they would value more systematic consultation in country, in the same vein as the country meetings which BMZ organises every year in Germany. Instituting an annual roundtable would be mutually beneficial.

Results and accountability

Stronger focus on results in designing and implementing technical and financial co-operation programmes

Germany takes a pragmatic approach to results and has good monitoring systems in programmes. The GIZ and KfW country teams in Mozambique and Kenya confirmed that the results matrix that BMZ is now using as a basis for commissioning programmes helps clarify expectations and focus attention on what can be achieved. These matrices use data and systems from national plans, minimising the need for additional indicators, separate data collection and parallel reporting requirements. GIZ and KfW define results for their programmes in terms of outcomes and outputs, while taking into account how their intervention may contribute to achieve higher-level development objectives. They also consider other action needed and constraining factors, as defined in national sector plans.

GIZ and KfW design their individual programmes within a joint programme proposal, around a common objective normally defined in the country strategy, which helps to ensure mutually reinforcing action. Several stakeholders raised concerns about the shorter duration of technical co-operation programmes, which are now limited to three years (compared to six years previously) and their mismatch with longer-term financial co-operation programmes, which can run for up to seven years. These differences in programme duration could undermine the scope for achieving synergies between technical and co-operation programmes. They could also increase transaction costs, since redesigning several programmes one after the other is less efficient than having one single longer, but phased, programme. In fact, GIZ programmes play a useful role in preparing the ground for financial co-operation programmes. However, if technical co-operation ends before financial co-operation starts, this can reduce the potential impact of financial co-operation. Moreover, the shorter duration of technical co-operation programmes may not be conducive to the long-term perspective needed to build national capacities and ensure sustainability. GIZ and KfW, however, are dealing pragmatically with these constraints, as they can anticipate potential future programming on the basis of Germany's long-term engagement in focus sectors. Also, the introduction of country strategies, which cover two programming cycles of government-to-government negotiations, will increase predictability in the future.

A more systematic portfolio review would enhance strategic decision making

In Kenya and Mozambique, evidence from evaluations and strategic analysis could do more to inform programming choices. While GIZ and KfW commission independent project evaluations, a more systematic portfolio review could help BMZ to base future strategic choices on the effectiveness of its approaches rather than existing programmes. Although Germany's long-term engagement in focus sectors brings reliability and experience, it is not always clear if BMZ has enough evidence to assess whether the selection of priorities and programmes within these sectors is relevant and effective enough to achieve the desired results. Periodic portfolio evaluations would enhance Germany's ability to assess the overall effectiveness of its co-operation in a country, and to inform future programming choices without being unduly influenced by current involvement.

Germany helps strengthen partners' monitoring and evaluation systems

Most German technical co-operation programmes include a component for strengthening the monitoring and evaluation systems of partner governments. As part of its support to the education sector in Mozambique, GIZ has developed "POEMA", a programme on integrated public management, enabling the ministry to better plan, prepare budget, manage resources, and conduct monitoring and evaluation. Other ministries have adopted the tools developed under this programme. In its decentralisation programme, GIZ supports districts in adopting and using governance and service delivery indicators.

In Kenya, German support in focus sectors includes an institutional development component. In the water sector, such institutional support has led the Water Services Regulatory Board to report annually on the government's performance in service delivery.

ORGANISATION FOR ECONOMIC CO-OPERATION AND DEVELOPMENT

The OECD is a unique forum where governments work together to address the economic, social and environmental challenges of globalisation. The OECD is also at the forefront of efforts to understand and to help governments respond to new developments and concerns, such as corporate governance, the information economy and the challenges of an ageing population. The Organisation provides a setting where governments can compare policy experiences, seek answers to common problems, identify good practice and work to co-ordinate domestic and international policies.

The OECD member countries are: Australia, Austria, Belgium, Canada, Chile, the Czech Republic, Denmark, Estonia, Finland, France, Germany, Greece, Hungary, Iceland, Ireland, Israel, Italy, Japan, Korea, Luxembourg, Mexico, the Netherlands, New Zealand, Norway, Poland, Portugal, the Slovak Republic, Slovenia, Spain, Sweden, Switzerland, Turkey, the United Kingdom and the United States. The European Commission takes part in the work of the OECD.

OECD Publishing disseminates widely the results of the Organisation's statistics gathering and research on economic, social and environmental issues, as well as the conventions, guidelines and standards agreed by its members.

DEVELOPMENT ASSISTANCE COMMITTEE

To achieve its aims, the OECD has set up a number of specialised committees. One of these is the Development Assistance Committee (DAC), whose mandate is to promote development co-operation and other policies so as to contribute to sustainable development – including pro-poor economic growth, poverty reduction and the improvement of living standards in developing countries – and to a future in which no country will depend on aid. To this end, the DAC has grouped the world's main donors, defining and monitoring global standards in key areas of development.

The members of the DAC are Australia, Austria, Belgium, Canada, the Czech Republic, Denmark, the European Union, Finland, France, Germany, Greece, Iceland, Ireland, Italy, Japan, Korea, Luxembourg, the Netherlands, New Zealand, Norway, Poland, Portugal, the Slovak Republic, Slovenia, Spain, Sweden, Switzerland, the United Kingdom and the United States.

The DAC issues guidelines and reference documents in the DAC Guidelines and Reference Series to inform and assist members in the conduct of their development co-operation programmes.

OECD PUBLISHING, 2, rue André-Pascal, 75775 PARIS CEDEX 16
(43 2015 09 1 P) ISBN 978-92-64-24612-6 – 2015-01

www.ingramcontent.com/pod-product-compliance
Lightning Source LLC
Chambersburg PA
CBHW081126180926
51611CB00004B/65
9789264246126